Cooperative Learning Throughout the Curriculum

Together We Learn Better

by

Sharon Rybak

illustrated by
Gary Mohrmann

Cover by Gary Mohrmann

Copyright © Good Apple, 1992

ISBN No. 0-86653-664-7

Printing No. 987654

Good Apple
1204 Buchanan St., Box 299
Carthage, IL 62321-0299

S I M O N & S C H U S T E R *A Paramount Communications Company*

DEDICATION

This book is dedicated to my wonderful class of second graders. Each of you, every day helps me to be a better teacher. You have taken my idea of personal ownership for your education and made it a reality. You work very hard because you want to learn. You don't do it for Mom or Dad, for grades or for me. You work hard because it is for you! My wish for your future is that you will carry the seeds of ownership for your learning to grow into lifelong learners. My respect for each of you is unending, and forever you will hold an important place in my heart. From Mrs. Rybak with love,

Miss Nicole Betor
Miss Ashley Berger
Miss Megan Arrick
Mr. Christopher Eyring
Mr. Michael Dorenkott
Mr. Chris Schafer
Miss Lisa Geiger
Miss Rachel Jerome
Mr. Matthew Mayo
Mr. Matt Stahoviak
Miss Maria Souris
Miss Casey Merriman
Mr. Michael Klidas
Miss Amber Williams
Miss Katherine Peoples
Miss Melissa Rocco
Mr. Derick Bronish
Mr. Mark Derian
Mr. Kyle Schlosser
Miss Yvonne Buemi
Mr. Reed Hazen
Miss Sarah Morgan

GA1396

TABLE OF CONTENTS

GA1396

TO THE READER

The first pages of this book are the rationale for my approach to teaching children. The remainder of this book is the fun stuff that can be done with children to create a classroom of motivated learners. Please remember that the goal for the teacher is to act as a facilitator of learning.

COOPERATIVE LEARNING IS MORE THAN GAMES AND ACTIVITIES IN CONTRIVED GROUPS WITH REWARDS FOR GOOD WORK SKILLS. COOPERATIVE LEARNING IS AN ATTITUDE OF RESPECT FOR THE STUDENT'S CAPACITY TO LEARN, TO TEACH AND TO CONTRIBUTE TO THE ENTIRE CLASS.

CHILDREN WHO LEARN IN THIS ENVIRONMENT TAKE THE FIRST STEPS TO BECOMING LIFELONG LEARNERS BECAUSE THEY EXPERIENCE OWNERSHIP, INITIATIVE AND AN INTRINSIC MOTIVATION TO LEARN.

A CLOSE LOOK AT GROUP WORK

Working, talking and interaction with another human being in a classroom used to be called cheating. For most teachers, their own upbringing in schools was directed around the familiar teacher remark, "Do your own work!" Teachers tried their best to get children to work alone, but the most frequently asked question in American schools is one child asking another, "What are we supposed to do?"

It is natural to turn to a fellow student for direction, and it is natural for people to work together. Schools have seemed to work in counterproduction to this idea for some valid reasons. The reasoning was as follows:

1. Some students would not do the required work and would ride on the accomplishments of the other students.

2. Talented students would do the work and take over for less able students.

3. Individual assessment was difficult to collect.

4. Working groups caused children to display off task behaviors.

To understand the concept of group work, teachers need to take another look at their belief systems. Here are some questions to ask yourself to explore your beliefs about children and learning. Take the time to think about your answers to these questions.

1. Do children learn best in a quiet, isolated environment?

2. Are test scores and individual grades of a student's skills the best indications of a child's growth?

3. Why do children come to school? What are their goals?

4. Should children be involved in each other's learning?

5. Can student motivation have an effect on the problems associated with group process?

GA1396

BREAKING DOWN THE OLD WAYS OF THINKING ABOUT LEARNING

Children learn in a variety of ways and under a variety of conditions. Prior to entering a school environment, children have learned in an extremely disorganized manner. Schools of the past put an end to that disorganization and attempted to put order into learning.

Before coming to school children learned "on the job." They were taught a little something by everyone they met along the way. They generally learned the most from the people they liked the most. In particular, the learning of language is a messy deal. After the first cheers for "Mama" and "Dada," most children are expected to just "pick it up." The complicated syntax of language is learned without a grammar lesson. How do children learn to say "That is my red truck" instead of saying "That's my truck red"? We come to realize that children have had many complex lessons in a very disorganized manner and yet they learn quite proficiently. There are some things we know about the disorganization.

1. Children are involved with a variety of people, and through that interaction they learn. In isolation, children cannot learn.

2. Children have a tolerance for being immersed in something. They thrive in environments with lots of stimulation.

3. Children have an internal motivator that helps them want to learn. They will fall repeatedly and still learn to walk and will struggle to communicate their needs through repeated requests.

4. Children are familiar with learning from a variety of individuals. They learn from siblings, family, neighbors and friends.

5. Children are capable of learning without being taught the breakdown of individual skills.

6. Children have their own intrinsic purpose which is to learn.

Schools have to look at this success story and wonder about our past directions in the pursuit of learning. Did we truly understand the learner, or did we create schools to accommodate the institution of school?

CHILDREN MUST DESIRE AN EDUCATION IN ORDER TO RECEIVE ONE

Our goals should be modest and yet grand. Our students should be as motivated to learn as they were when they were young children. After all, there are no teachers without learners. Teachers cannot pour knowledge into children's ears, nor can they cover their eyes with information and skills if the students are not ready to receive. Children must desire an education in order to receive one.

What motivates people? What gives them satisfaction? The lowest level of satisfaction comes from receiving something for a job completed. In school we give stickers, put stamps on papers and give grades. In the real world we receive a paycheck for our work. To work for a paycheck or a grade is a very low level of intrinsic worth. People who get out of bed, drive to work and spend their day in the pursuit of a paycheck work on a low level of job-related satisfaction.

The next level of worth is to work for the result of the job itself. We may not like all the details along the way, but we derive satisfaction in seeing the end product. The result may not be a product, but a goal reached at the conclusion of a job well done. That provides motivation for the long, hard journey.

One of the highest levels of intrinsic worth is for people to find satisfaction in a job and internal motivation because the process was worth doing in and of itself. Another way of looking at this is that it was the right thing to do. This is the level at which most young children operate. They want to learn because it feels right.

Why do young learners lose that internal motivation to learn? What is absent from the school process that condones children doing just enough to get by?

We all want motivated students. Teachers want motivated students, parents want motivated students, school boards and administrations want motivated students, but nobody seems to be able to identify the elements of this elusive human quality for students.

GA1396

OWNERSHIP

My parents had a hand-pushed lawn mower when I was a child. As I got older, they would try to get me to mow their grass. I hated the job, and I'm sure I let my feelings be known. I remember thinking that it wasn't my grass. If they wanted a house with a lawn, they should mow it themselves. I had no ownership feelings toward that lawn.

Years later my husband and I bought our first home. That first summer we worked on the yard with diligence. I can remember the feeling I had as I finished mowing the front lawn. I remember reflecting on how different I felt because it was mine. I owned the lawn. I took pride in its beauty, and I felt satisfaction in every element of the process. Why did I feel so different? I enjoyed the job because it belonged to me. I chose the job and I loved the final product.

Ownership motivates and makes the workers feel a level of satisfaction. In millions of ways we steal ownership away from children. Parents and teachers need to realize that children have a right to own their education. They need to feel as if they are working for themselves, not to please parents or teachers. Bumper stickers that say "My Child Is on the Honor Roll at Sunshine High" are really saying "Didn't I do a good job as a parent?" Why doesn't the sticker say, "I'm on the Honor Roll at Sunshine High and Proud of It"? In many subtle ways we take power away from children.

Ownership is very powerful when it comes from a group of individuals. As each member of the group takes ownership, the group becomes more effective, efficient and productive. We need only to look at America to see that our best moments came when we had unity and a joint vision.

ESTABLISHING THE OBJECTIVE

Ask your children why they came to school. There is usually only one answer, "To learn." Ask your children every morning, "Why did you come to school today?" Encourage everyone to answer with a rousing rendition of "To learn." The first objective has been established, and it has been vocalized. It is important that children say this out loud. It helps them program their minds to the purpose at hand. They have made the commitment to themselves to learn. This is a very powerful technique to use with children.

I tell my children that learning is here for them to take or throw away. If they choose to throw it away, do it quietly.

GA1396

CHILDREN AS TEACHERS = MOTIVATION

One of the first lessons that needs to be taught to children is to discuss the difference between *teaching* and *telling*. We describe *telling* as giving someone the answer, and *teaching* as helping someone find the answer. The children are in a classroom to assist each other. If one child knows how to put together a puzzle, that child becomes the puzzle expert and helps others with the puzzle when they have difficulty.

Older children can instruct each other in a variety of ways. Once a question is answered by a teacher, the teacher can refer the next duplicated question to the child who received the answer. This gives the child the opportunity to teach what has just been learned.

My second grade students take on teaching responsibilities every day. If a child has been absent for a spelling test, then someone will administer the test. The children buddy study in every subject by asking each other questions. Children read and then discuss the reading. Specific questions allow them to explore issues and get excited about the ideas in group discussion. Cooperative learning is more than games and activities in contrived groups. It is an attitude of respect for the abilities of the learner and each child's capacity to teach and contribute to the class.

MAKING CHOICES

Motivation and satisfaction come from ownership, knowing your goals and assuming responsibilities, but the largest contributor to worker motivation is having choice.

America is built on the freedom of choice. Wars have been waged to secure our freedom to choose the way we want to live in the United States. We have the freedom to work and live where we want and say and do what we want within the framework of the laws of our land. Those choices give us initiative and motivation to be anything we want to be because we have control and power over our destiny.

What would happen if tomorrow we were to lose our ability to choose? The grocery would have one type of ice cream and one type of cereal. How would we feel if we were told what we were to do and when we were to do it? How much does our freedom of choice mean to us? I suspect a great deal.

GA1396

"BECAUSE I SAID SO"

Most of us remember being told this by our parents when we asked, "Why?" "Because I said so!" Most schools are run on this theory. Children have no input in their learning and complete tasks because they are told to. The simple element of choice put into this system allows the same activities to take place, but with an ownership and an enthusiasm by the learner.

Children need to be aware of the curriculum and have input into some of the decisions within reason. If teachers have a choice of which unit to complete first, why not allow input from the class?

Children can make simple choices about the number of times they write their spelling words. I encourage my children to write them as many times as it takes to remember them. Some hand them in written once, and others write them ten times.

Classrooms without freedom of choice create atmospheres where children may feel like prisoners. Children need opportunities to come out from under the guard's watchful eye and be allowed to explore, think, move and learn.

The fear of letting children make choices is that they might make wrong choices. Obviously, the choices that children can make need to be safe and protective, but not prohibitive of some failure. Children also learn from their mistakes.

CHASE VERSUS DRAG PHILOSOPHY

All of this leads to teachers who have to chase their students through the school year rather than having to drag them. Children are too heavy to drag, and it is nearly impossible to move someone who doesn't want to learn. The easiest and most efficient method is to create an environment that provides the essential elements of motivation.

initiative	choices
satisfaction	capacity to instruct
ownership	respect
goal setting	belonging

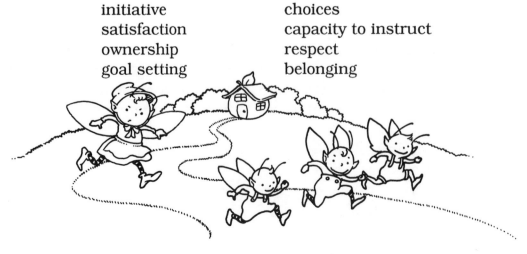

GA1396

ELEMENTS OF WORKING GROUPS FOR YOUNG CHILDREN

Children enjoy the opportunity to work with each other in the learning process. Children can work in groups of two to five or even six, depending on the activity. Groups can also encompass the entire classroom full of children depending on the desired outcome. The teacher needs to take careful stock of the activity and decide how that group will work together and what is the optimum number of participants.

ALL CHILDREN NEED SOMETHING IN THEIR HANDS

Young children do not share well. If one child has the crayons or paper, then the other children will be preoccupied with the thoughts of getting the crayons and paper. Even if the children have learned to control their feelings and refrain from fighting over objects, most young children will be absorbed with the thoughts of getting their turn.

To avoid this, try to give something to everyone in the group. If children have to share a paper, then make sure that it is shared between no more than two people. Giving in to the need for children to have their own belongings seems to go in counterproduction to cooperative learning. Children's need for territory is very basic and shouldn't have to be fought over except in the extreme cases. Children can learn to be cooperative once they have established that everyone has had a FAIR start.

WHO SHOULD WORK WITH WHOM?

There is always a recommendation in every class to keep two particular children apart. They talk too much, fight too much, tease each other or just can't seem to get along. It is important for the teacher to assess each situation individually. Children may be denied valuable lessons if they are always grouped with children of similar temperament.

Some children want to work together all the time. As soon as groups are decided, these two individuals are stuck together like glue. I have found that it may be a good idea to let these two work together until they get tired of the relationship. Teacher separation of children who have deep desires to work together sometimes causes more problems than it solves.

Some children have difficult times with groups. They may be reticent or overly bossy. Some children don't know how to proceed with a work situation if other children are watching. Teachers need to monitor each individual and give the children an opportunity to express their feelings and share their frustrations.

DEBRIEFING

After a group session, it is important to ask the children for their input. Children can learn a great deal by giving their opinions and ideas for the future. Doing the debriefing may seem time consuming, but it is through these discussions that children learn to evaluate and change.

With young children, the groups will be together for a short duration, and the problems may need ongoing discussion with the group as the teacher roams around the classroom. Positive comments for quality work should be frequent, and the children should be monitored for frustration. Problems may pop up throughout the classroom, and it is at that moment the teacher must decide the role he/she should play.

If the children are to have ownership for the activity, then the teacher needs to let them own the problem. This is the moment that true learning takes place. The teacher's comments need to be general and open-ended to let the students make some decisions about the problem.

Teacher: How did your work come along today?
Group: We didn't get done.
Teacher: Why do you think you had trouble getting done?
Amanda: We kept fighting over who would get to do the puzzle.
Teacher: How do you feel about not getting done?
David: I told them that we should do it this way.
Amanda: That wasn't going to work, David!
Teacher: Well, this does seem to be a problem. What do you think would help?
Margaret: David and Amanda fought the whole time and hogged the puzzle.
Teacher: I think David and Amanda were trying to get the job done. What could they have done differently?

This leads the children on to a series of possibilities for the next conflict situation. If the children don't have any ideas for conflict resolution, then the teacher can make some suggestions and then ask the children's opinions of these various techniques.

AN INTRODUCTION TO COOPERATIVE LEARNING FOR CHILDREN

What If the Three Little Pigs Had Cooperated?

GA1396

BUILD IT TOGETHER

The story "The Three Little Pigs" gives children an opportunity to work in groups and re-create their own version of the story. This unit includes the following materials:

The story of The Three Little Pigs
Mama Pig puppet
Sam the Pig puppet
Fred the Pig puppet
Max the Pig puppet
Big Bad Wolf

House of Sticks
House of Straw
Max's Mansion

The Three Little Pigs Poem
The Untold Story–A Rebus Buddy Activity
An Advertisement for Pig Protection
No Wolves Street Sign
Precious Pig Players Award

The materials can be used in a variety of ways. Their purpose is to give children opportunities to work in groups of two to four.

Ideas for Using the Pig Puppets

- Create storytelling groups. The teacher can assign the groups or the children can self-select.

- The puppets can be copied onto tagboard or backed with cardboard. They could also be used on paper bags. The puppets can be supported with sticks or rulers. The puppets can also be glued to stuffed paper bags that are supported with rulers or sticks.

- The houses are designed to cover the outsides of half-gallon milk or juice containers. The children can decorate the outsides and the insides of the houses. The houses can be run on tagboard to make them more sturdy for the added weight of the decorations. The fronts of the houses can be used alone or decorated and mounted on sticks for simple props.

The House of Straw: Decorate with thin strips of gold construction paper, yellow Easter grass, or shredded wheat cereal.

The House of Sticks: Decorate with thin pretzels or pieces of brown paper bags cut into strips.

The House of Bricks: Cut a potato and use it as a stamper with a red stamp pad, or glue on small red rectangular pieces of paper.

GA1396

THE THREE LITTLE PIGS PLAY

- The children should work in groups no larger than four. Mama and the Wolf can be one child; three other children can be Sam, Fred and Max.

- Let the children have freedom to create and re-create the story without a written text. Encourage innovation on the original story.

- Be careful to steer the children away from violence and toward a cooperative solution for the pigs.

- Children need time to create the scenery, characters and props and to practice.

- Let each group perform their rendition for the other class members.

- Award the children the Precious Pig Players Award for a perfect performance.

THE THREE LITTLE PIGS STORY

Once upon a time, many years ago there lived a mother pig who had three piglets. They were very pink and soft. Mama named them Fred, Sam and Max. Mama loved her sweet little piglets, but there was only one problem. The piglets were always pushing each other away from the food when it was time to eat. The piglets would fight for the best mud, and snort and push for the best straw in the pen. But the worse fights were over the food. The piglets would fight so much, that Mama would have to put the pigs in the corners of the pigpen and give them a time out.

Now the pigs loved to eat, and they never did stop their fighting over everything. They kept growing and eating and growing and eating until they were bigger than their mother. There was no place left to move in the pigpen, and Mama knew it was time for her three piglets to find their own homes.

Fred decided that he would like a house of straw. "Straw is good because I can roll up against it and scratch my back," he said.

Mama looked at Fred and felt sad. He was still her baby even if he did weigh 380 pounds. She told him, "Fred, you must be careful because outside this pigpen you might just meet the Big Bad Wolf."

Fred looked at his mother the way piglets do and said, "Aw, Ma, who's afraid of the Big Bad Wolf? Sam and Max, are you coming with me?"

Well, Max and Sam looked at Fred, and they shook their little piggy heads "no." "We want our own food, and besides, who ever heard of a house made of straw!" said the brothers.

"Can't you boys ever agree on anything?" asked Mama. But she had to agree that a house of straw was not enough protection to keep away the Big Bad Wolf.

Well, who should be watching from the nearby forest but the Big Bad Wolf. This is just what he had hoped would happen. If they stayed together, he could never catch them; but if they were apart, he knew he would soon be eating piggy pork stew for his supper.

Sam fancied himself as being smarter than his brothers, and he decided to build his house of mud and sticks. "Sticks are good because they will keep me warm when the cold wind blows," he said.

"Sticks are no protection from the Big Bad Wolf, because I have heard that he can huff and puff a house of sticks to the ground," said Mama. "Remember that the Big Bad Wolf loves to eat fat piggies."

Sam didn't consider himself fat; he only weighed 420 pounds.

4

GA1396

Both Fred and Sam looked at Max. A part of them felt happy to be grown-up and on their own, but a part of them was sad because they knew that they would miss all the fussing and fighting.

"What are you going to do, Max?" asked the brothers.

"I'm going over the hill and read books about building the biggest, strongest and safest house you have ever seen," said Max.

"Are you afraid of the Big Bad Wolf?" teased Fred and Sam.

"No...," said Max.

"Max is afraid of the Big Bad Wolf, Big Bad Wolf, Big Bad Wolf!" chanted the brothers.

Sadly, Max walked away over the hill, leaving his family behind.

Now as you know, the Big Bad Wolf was watching all of this from the forest. He watched as Fred built his house of straw and then watched as Sam built his house of sticks. He didn't know what happened to Max, because he was on the other side of the hill. The wolf decided to try the house of straw first because it was the easiest to huff and puff to the ground.

"Little pig, little pig, let me in," said the wolf.

Fred looked out the window and said in his strongest, fiercest voice, "Not by the hair on my chinny chin-chin, I won't let you in. Go away."

But you know what the wolf said. Let's say it together. "Then I'll huff and I'll puff and I'll blow your house in."

Fred had to think fast. He pushed against the back wall of his house and made a quick getaway just as he heard the sound of the straw house tumbling to the wolf's huffing and puffing.

Fred was a fat little pig, and he had to do some huffing and puffing of his own to run to his brother's house.

Meanwhile, the wolf was digging through the straw looking for the pig. He soon realized that Fred had escaped.

Fred ran to the door of the house of sticks and rushed in. He quickly told Sam that the wolf was on his way. Both little piggies were wondering about their brother. Each little pig stuck his snout through the slots in the sticks and peaked out. Their little curly tails shook with fear.

The wolf walked up to the house of sticks and he was angry. This time he said in a much meaner voice, "Little pigs, little pigs, let me in." Together the brothers chanted, "Not by the hair on our chinny chin-chins, we won't let you in. Go away."

GA1396

But, you know what the wolf said. Let's say it together. "Then I'll huff and I'll puff and I'll blow your house in."

Fred and Sam had to think fast. They pushed against the back wall of the house and made a quick getaway, just as they heard the sound of the stick house tumbling to the wolf's huffing and puffing.

Fred and Sam were fat little pigs, and they had to do some huffing and puffing of their own to run to their brother's house. But the pigs could not see their brother's house, and they weren't sure where to find him. Meanwhile, the wolf was digging through the sticks looking for the pigs. He soon realized that Fred and Sam had escaped.

Fred and Sam now knew that they must work together to find their brother. As they crossed the hill, they saw a forest and beyond the forest, they saw a hill, and on the hill in the far off distance they saw a small figure that looked like their brother, Max. Sam and Fred traveled by hoof for three days and three nights. Whatever they found to eat they shared without a fight. The brothers knew that they needed each other.

Finally, on the third day, the pigs came out of the forest and saw the hill with a huge house of bricks sitting on the very top. There was a bright neon sign that was flashing at the very top that said "Max's Mansion." The brothers felt happy to be so near their brother's safe home. As they got closer, they saw a sign that said "No Wolves." The brothers crossed the moat by walking over a narrow bridge and knocked on the huge front door of the mansion. Suddenly lights went on and bells began to ring, and the brothers held each other and began to cry. A small window opened and Max stuck out his snout. Sam and Fred would know that snout anywhere and began to yell with glee.

"Let us in. The Big Bad Wolf is trying to catch us."

"How do I know you are my brothers and not the Big Bad Wolf?" asked Max.

Sam and Fred had to think. "Remember the time you ate too much food and couldn't get out of the mud for a week?" said the brothers.

Max opened the door, and the three brothers were together again.

"There are lots of things we can do that will protect us from the Big Bad Wolf," said Max.

"I can make a fence of sticks," said Sam.

"I can make a trap with straw," said Fred. The three brothers knew that from this day forward they would work together to solve their problems.

Years later Grandma Pig would tell the story of the Three Little Pigs to her grand piglets. They never got tired of hearing the story of their daddies and the Big Bad Wolf.

6

GA1396

7

SAM PIG

8

GA1396

FRED PIG

9

MAX PIG

10

BIG BAD WOLF

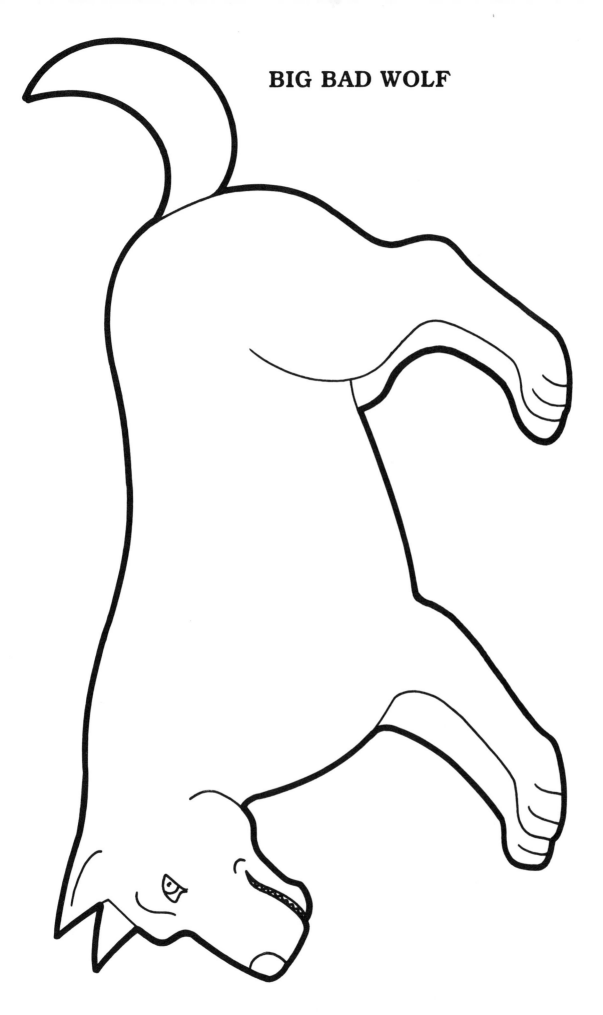

11

HOUSE OF STRAW

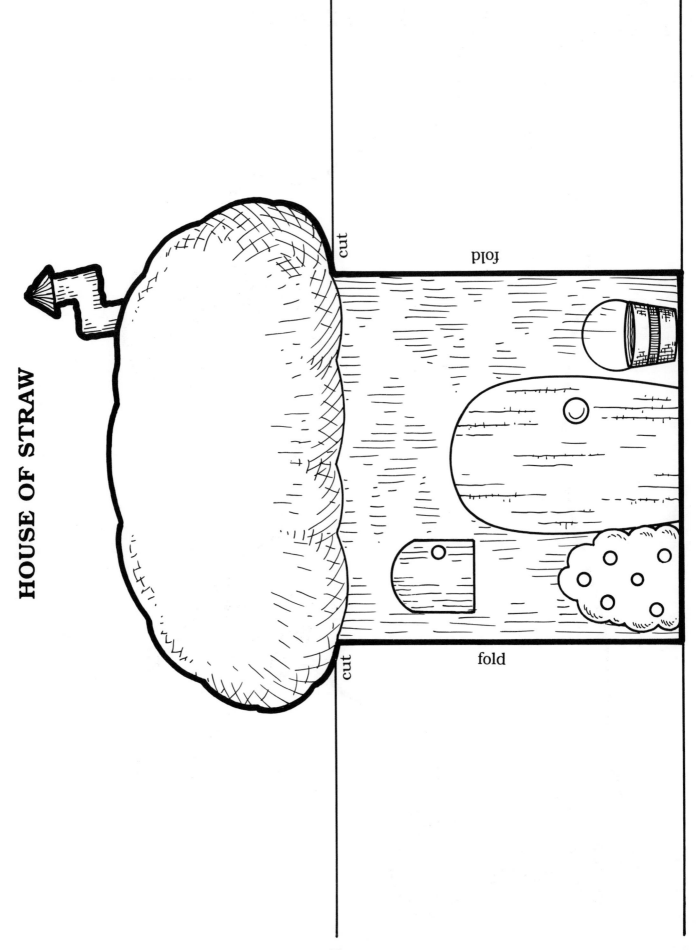

cut

fold

cut

fold

12

GA1396

HOUSE OF STICKS

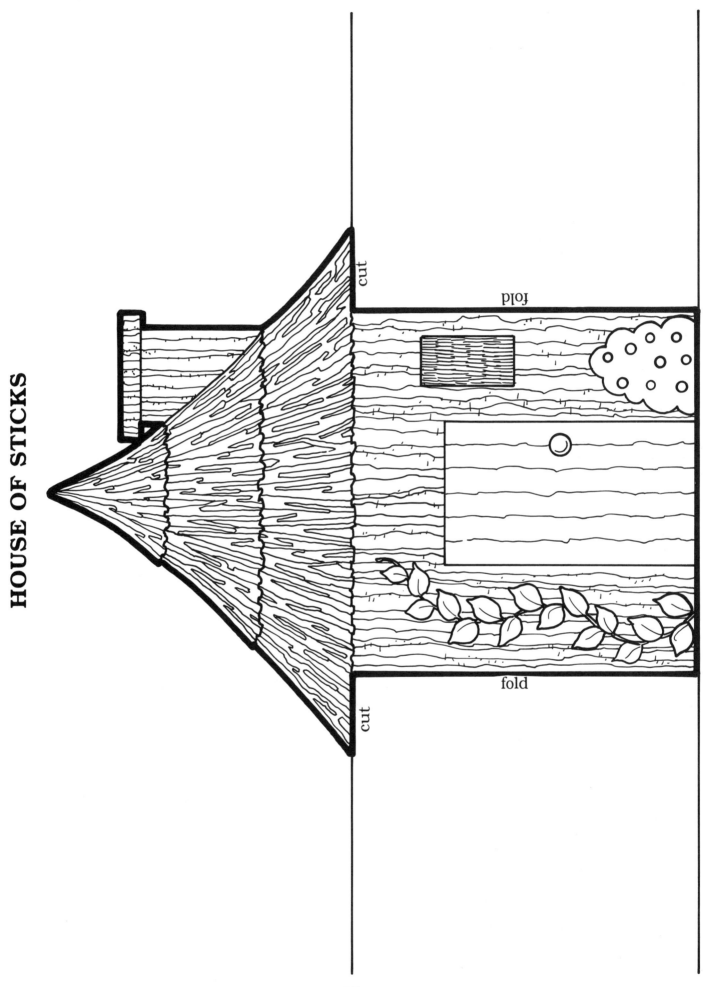

cut

fold

cut

fold

GA1396

MAX'S MANSION

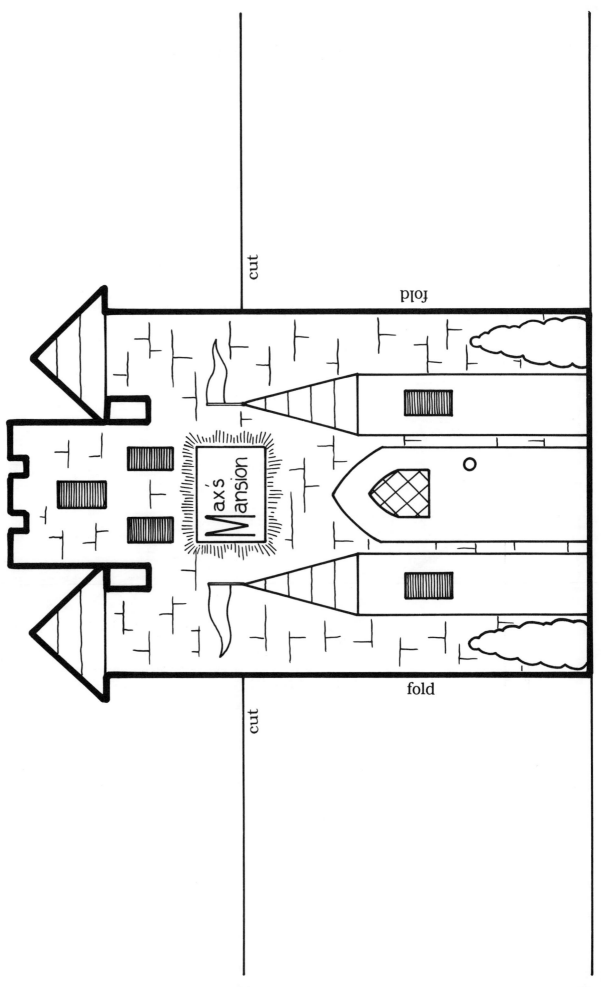

14

GA1396

THE UNTOLD STORY

Max cried for [ ] days after he left his [ ] and

two brothers. He would show them! He was going to build the

biggest, strongest and safest [ ] in the [ ] . He

went to the [ ] to read [ ] about building safe

houses. He decided to use [ ] to build his house. Max

got [ ] for the cement, and he worked hard to build his

[ ] . Max also put up a [ ] that warned the

[ ] to stay away.

When Max was done, he put up a large neon sign that

said ☐ just in case his ☐ came to find him.

One day, Max heard a knock on the front ☐ . He was

afraid because he thought it was the ☐ . Max hit the

alarm system and ☐ went on and ☐ began to

ring. When Max opened the door, he saw it was ☐ and

☐ . Together again, they stopped their fussing and fight-

ing and lived happily ever after.

GA1396

DOUBLE BUDDY REBUS PICTURE
THE THREE LITTLE PIGS–THE UNTOLD STORY

Buddy 1

| The End | lights | library | books | bricks |
| neon sign | Fred | three | house | door |

Buddy 2

| Mama Pig | house | cement truck | no wolves | wolf |
| brothers | bells | Sam | Big Bad Wolf | world |

Cut and paste pictures for the rebus story, The Untold Story.

THE THREE LITTLE PIGS POEM

The three little pigs
Built their houses alone.
No one to help them
No one to phone.

But Fred and Sam
Had a very great scare.
The Big Bad Wolf
Left them nothing to spare.

So they ran to see Max,
And he did what he could
To protect his brothers
From the Big Bad Wolf.

So remember the lesson;
Together it's fun.
Work hard and cooperate;
United they won!

18

WOLVES CAN'T READ

Create a sign that doesn't need any words, but will tell the Big Bad Wolf to stay away from the Three Little Pigs.

ADVERTISEMENT

Create an advertisement for something that will protect the Three Little Pigs. Think about fences, alarms, locks, lights and warning systems. Be creative!

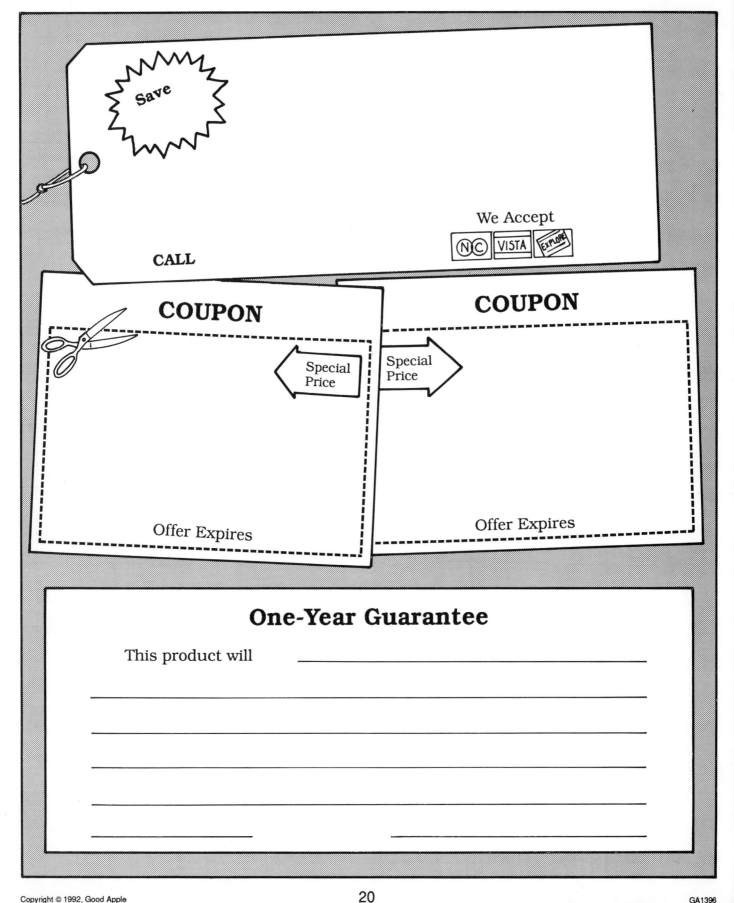

Save

We Accept

CALL

COUPON

Special Price

Offer Expires

COUPON

Special Price

Offer Expires

One-Year Guarantee

This product will _____

_____

_____

_____

_____

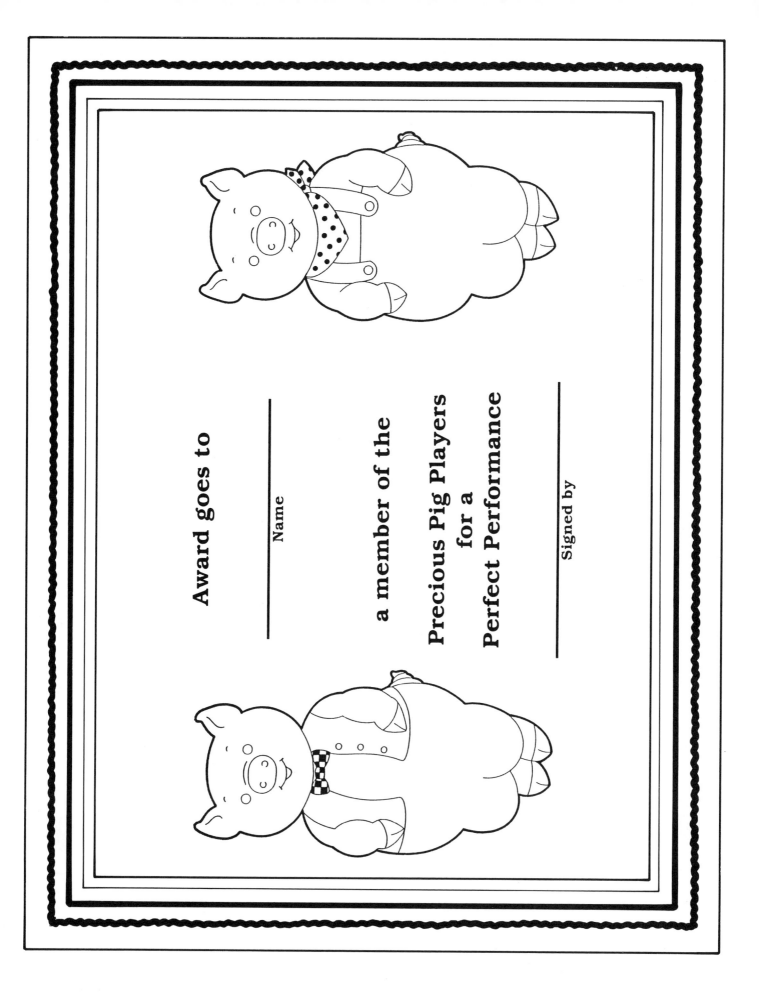

Award goes to

_____
Name

a member of the

Precious Pig Players
for a
Perfect Performance

_____
Signed by

21

PROMOTING BUDDY BUILDING IN THE AREAS OF READING, WRITING, MAP SKILLS AND ART

Jack and the Giant

22

BUDDY BUILDING
IN TWO-MEMBER TEAMS

This unit promotes buddy building between two children. Getting along with another individual can be a difficult task. This unit gives the children an opportunity to look at both sides of an issue and do interactive activities. The unit should begin with the children hearing or reading for themselves the story "Jack and the Beanstalk." Many excellent renditions of the story are available.

The following activities support the story theme.

Jack's Helpers
In this activity, the children read the poem and follow the clues to identify each of the buildings in the town of Big Time. Each child has part of the pieces, and together they need to complete one map. If each child wants a completed product, copies of the original can be made so each child will have one to take home.

Letters from Jack and the Giant
This format provides the children an opportunity to write letters back and forth as they assume the characters of the Giant and Jack. What would the Giant say to Jack, and how would Jack respond? If the children are prereaders, they can draw pictures for each other and dictate simple messages.

The Village Times
In this activity, the children write a news article from the home newspapers of both the Giant and Jack. It might be helpful to discuss the attitude that Jack would have and how the Giant might feel about his things being taken. These could also be used on the overhead and done with the entire class.

Giant People
One child lies on the paper while the other child draws. These shapes are then transformed into giants by the children. Together they color in their one giant (which is actually their size). These can also be stuffed with newspaper and stapled together with backing paper. These giants make a fun display in the hallway. Include little houses and people, as well as a beanstalk with a little boy up near the top.

GA1396

JACK'S HELPERS

Now let it be known
That this boy named Jack
Created mischief with
A sack on his back.

He took as many things
As he could find
Back to his mum who lived
under the vine.

When Jack came to town,
The townspeople knew
They didn't want Jack
To take their stuff, too.

Jack had to stay hidden
And sneak through the town.
He carried his sack
And he poked all around.

So Jack needs your help
To find his way home.
Follow the directions
So he won't be alone.

Directions

Read clues 1-12 and find the correct location for each building. Cut and paste with your partner.

1. Jack left the Giant's Castle which is on the corner of Jack's Path and Fe Fi Fo Fum Blvd.

2. He went north and stopped to buy some shoes at Foot Path and Giant Lane. Big Shoes for Big Guys didn't have anything that fit.

3. He went west to G Mart—a store with a little bit more and found a pair of shoes on sale.

4. Jack then went south to window-shop at Giant Mobiles on Fe Fi Fo Fum Blvd.

5. He was getting sort of hungry so he stopped in Dunk Those Donuts on Golden Egg Lane, but he could eat only one at a time.

6. When he was done, he quickly stopped at Little's Corner for some flowers for his friend in the hospital.

7. The hospital was all the way across town on Englishmen and Giant Lane, but Jack knew he couldn't leave without saying good-bye to the Giant's kind wife who was sick with a cold.

GA1396

8. Jack made his way across town on Giant Lane and almost got caught at the jail on Harp Alley and Giant Lane, but he quietly slipped into the hospital.

9. When Jack was done with his visit, the Giant's wife asked him to deliver some thank-you cards to Twin One and Twin Two on Green Garden Street. Jack was very careful as he delivered the letters, but the twins saw him from their upstairs window.

10. Jack made a quick getaway into the Garden for Giants which is west of the twins' home. This garden had giant flowers and trees which was good for hiding from the Giant police.

11, Finally, when night came, Jack made his way to the All Night Camping Equipment Store on Beanstalk Road. He couldn't leave without some safety rope and an ax, just in case.

12. Jack made it to the beanstalk as the clock struck twelve. By now you and your partner should have found each place Jack visited on his trip around the city.

Check with the code below to see if you were correct.

Hey, no peeking until you are all done! The Giant says so!

1. Giant's Castle
2. Big Shoes for Big Guys
3. G Mart
4. Giant Mobiles
5. Dunk Those Donuts
6. Tiny's Flowers
7. Giant Hospital
8. Fe Fi Fo Fum Police Department
9 and 10. Twin One and Twin Two
11. Garden for Giants
12. All Night Camping Equipment Store

GA1396

HELP JACK FIND HIS WAY BACK TO THE BEANSTALK

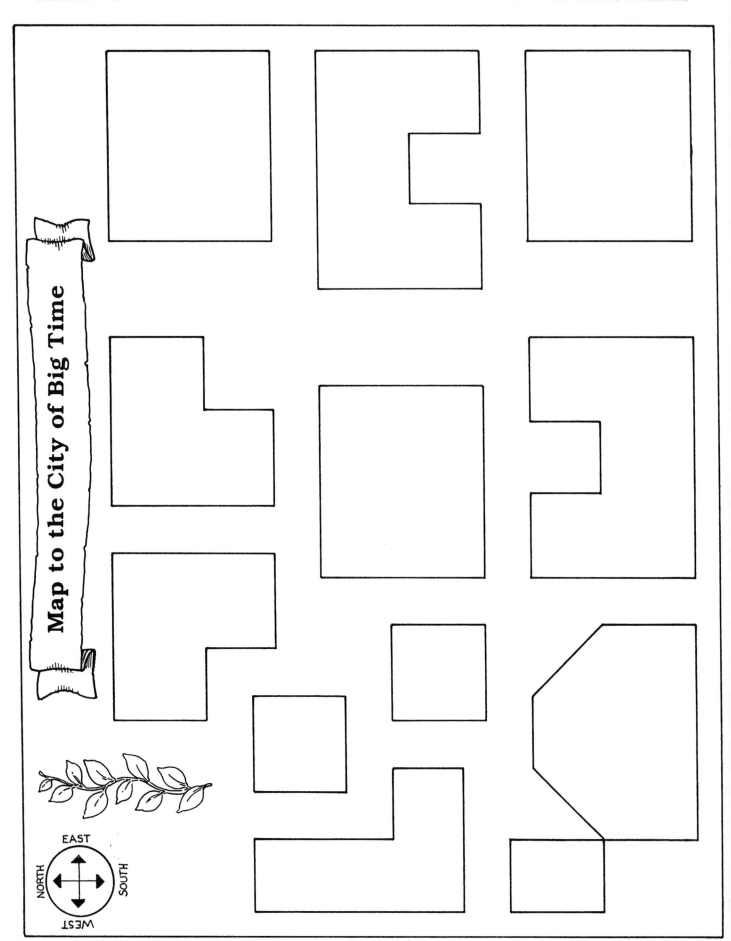

Map to the City of Big Time

EAST
NORTH
SOUTH
WEST

26

Helper 2

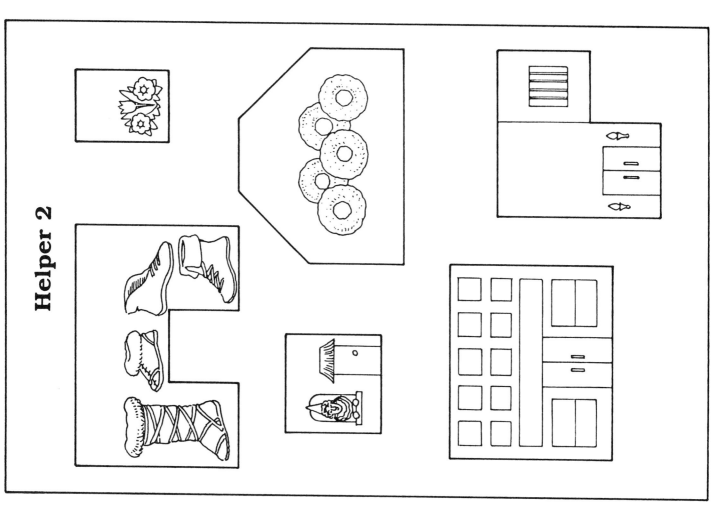

Helper 1

27

GA1396

LETTERS FROM
JACK AND THE GIANT

Dear Giant,	Dear Jack,
Dear Giant,	Dear Jack,
Dear Giant,	Dear Jack,

Student writing as the Giant

Student writing as Jack

The Village Times

Date _____

Giant No Match for Jack

Jack Tells His Story!

GA1396

The Fe Fi Fo Fum News

Date _____

Giant Tells His Story

Small Robber Gets Away

GA1396

COOPERATIVE ACTIVITIES IN SOCIAL STUDIES, SCIENCE, MATH, READING AND WRITING

Ants Understand That Together They Work Better

GA1396

ANTS HAVE LEARNED THAT TOGETHER THEY WORK BETTER

Ants are one of the most cooperative of all creatures on this Earth. Because they are so small, they depend on the strength they can achieve by working together. Man can learn many lessons by studying the habits of the ant.

Ant Farm

Uncle Milton's Ant Farms have long been some of the most popular science activities for children. In a very short time, the ants will create an entire community of dwellings, food storage units, and even a cemetery and hospital. Ants from the same colony do not fight and will work together for the common good. Units on communities and discussions on cooperation fit very nicely into the study of ants. Ants are known as the social insects.

Having a class ant farm is easy and inexpensive. The ants will have no chance of getting loose in the room environment. Children are fascinated by the movement of the ants. Best of all, the activity provides an opportunity to discuss the importance of their cooperation on the entire group's survival.

ADDRESS FOR: Uncle Milton's Ant Farm
P.O. Box 246
Culver City, California 90230

Ants Under the Big Top

The ant maze is to be completed by two children. They must work together and get their ants to the Big Top Circus. The puzzle is designed so the children will have to cross paths.

Ant Acrobatics

If you could train an ant, what tricks would you train your ant to do? The children get a chance to do some creative thinking about ant antics.

GA1396

Ant Circus Big Top

33

GA1396

 # ANT ACROBATICS

If you could train ants to do tricks. what tricks would you train them to do? Together with your partner decide on two tricks you would teach your ants. Draw a picture of your ants doing the tricks and decide on the problems you would have teaching your ants tricks.

Two tricks our ants could do.

1. _____

2. _____

Trick 1

Trick 2

These are problems we might have when training our ants.

_____

_____

_____

GA1396

ANT TREK GAME AND PUZZLE

The Ant Trek Game is designed to foster cooperation between four children. The initial step of the activity is to have the children actually create the gameboard. The puzzle has been divided into four sections. The children must discuss their puzzle parts and decide on the colors they will color for each section so they will match. If the children are readers, they can add details such as:

Miss one turn
Take an extra roll
Jump back one space
Crawl ahead two spaces
Take a swim and go back to go

The children should color and cut their puzzle parts and mount them on pieces of heavy tagboard. (This might need to be laminated or covered with clear plastic before beginning the game.) The children may want to add details of their own so they personalize the game. Here are some suggestions the teacher could help facilitate.

1. One team could be red ants and the other team black ants.
2. The ants could carry one toothpick which would save them from a dip in the water. Ants can give each other their toothpicks.
3. Plastic ants from novelty stores can be used.
4. Addition and subtraction facts could be used, and plastic ants could be used for counters. A correct answer must be given before going on to the next square.
5. Ant facts could also be used, such as the following:
   •The name given to the most important ant. (queen)
   •A home for a group of ants is called this name. (colony)
   •Ants can lift _____ times their weight. (50)
   •The name for ant eggs is this word. (larvae)

35

GA1396

ANT TREK

Game Rules

1. Number of players: Four players can play, with two players on each side of the water.

2. Object: Each ant will travel to the opposite island across the bridge.

3. Game Parts: Each player gets an ant marker.

4. Rules: Each player rolls one die and moves up either tree and over the bridge. Follow the ropes and arrows. If you land in the water, swim back to your original island. Watch for shortcuts and trips into the water. The first player to reach the other island wins.

Variations

Depending on the class reading level, various skills can be placed into the squares of the game. The following math story problems can be cut and pasted into the puzzle.

Two ants went hiking and three ants joined them. How many ants were there total?

Seven ants started to eat the leftover picnic food, but three got scared away. How many ants were left?

The anteater chased the nine ants and sadly, caught two. How many ants got away?

The ants had a parade. Five joined the seven that were already there. How many total were there?

If six ants stole some birthday cake and four ants got to eat it, how many ants missed the treat?

Five ants had a party for the queen. Seven ants attended. How many were at the party? Don't forget the queen.

GA1396

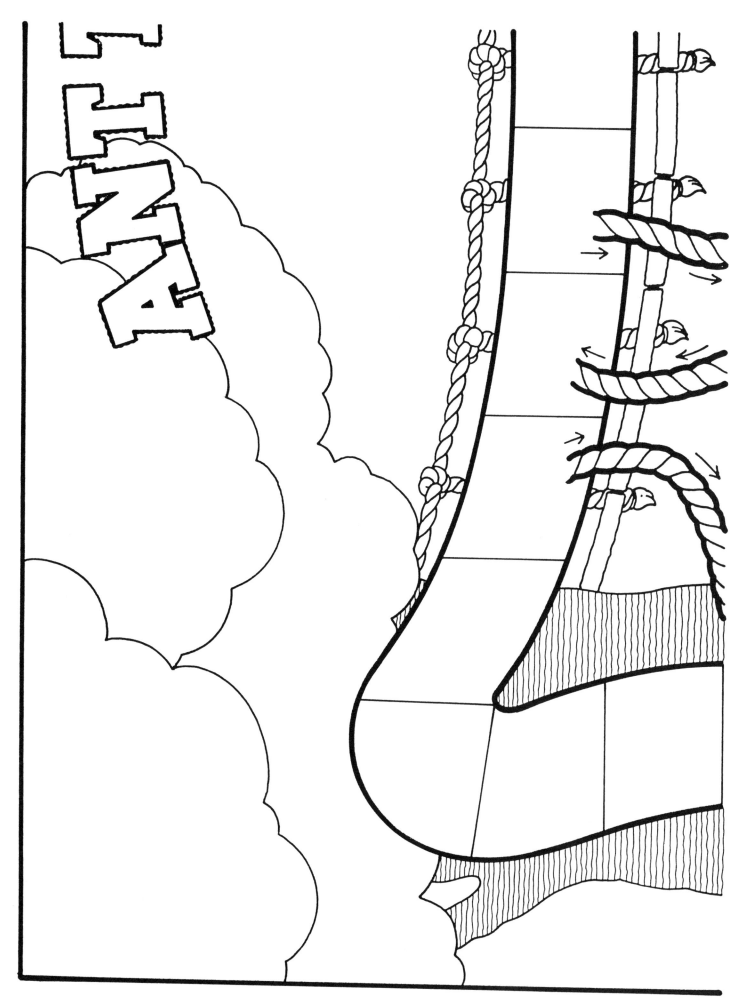

37

GA1396

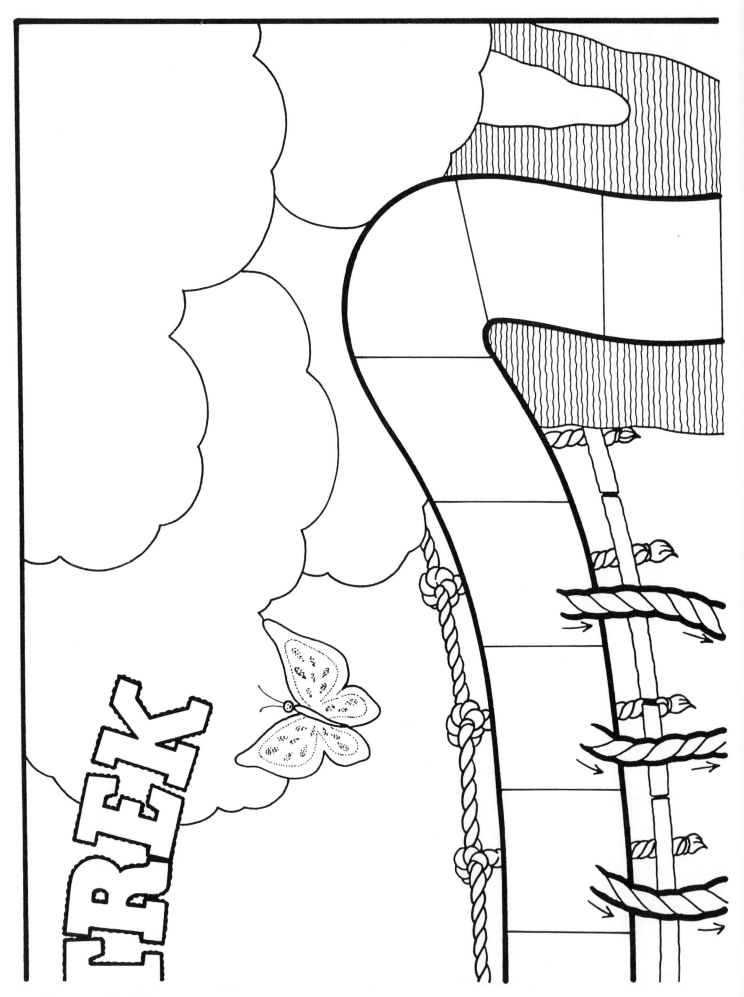

39

SHARED READING
ACTIVITIES

41

READING BUDDIES INTRODUCTION

Children take to the idea of buddy reading with great enthusiasm. I have found that children will spend more time with the task and do a better job on their reading assignments when they have a buddy for support. Below I will address a few of the issues that arise when children are buddy readers.

Getting a Partner
I give this advice from personal experience–let the children pick their own reading partners. When I have assigned the groups, the children seem stiff and uncomfortable. They need time to get acquainted. When the children pick their own partners, they seem to have that established bond, and the motivation is high.

Bosom Buddies
What happens when children get too carried away with the idea of a partner and refuse to stay on task? The teacher then separates the children, forcing them to work alone. On the next opportunity, ask them if they are ready to work together. Continue to let them make choices and accept the consequences and rewards for those choices. Don't assume the responsibility for children's off-task behavior by taking over. Allow the children to make the choices and reinforce the rules and the rewards.

What Should Buddies Do?
Children can read easy material two times, which gives each child an opportunity to read and hear the material. In most reading groups, children spend a small amount of time actually reading, but with this method they get to do more oral reading. The teacher can be moving from group to group during this time, visiting with each group, listening to their reading and asking questions.

Understanding the Content
Even the youngest of children can tell each other about their favorite part of the story. The following formats give the children an opportunity to work together to overview the book they have read. It may be helpful to give each child a sheet, even though the child has to fill in only his/her half of the information. Children may have difficulty sharing one piece of paper at first.

Story Prediction
Reading buddies can look at the cover and pictures in a book to see if they can predict what will happen in the story. The work sheet gives the children an opportunity for pre-reading book discussion.

Prereaders
Can children who are not yet reading be reading buddies? You bet they can. These little folks pick their favorite book and "read" it to their buddy. The work sheet allows the children an opportunity to put closure on the activity and give it more meaning.

GA1396

Where Do Children Read?

Children can read anywhere. I have seen children stand and read, sit two in a rocking chair and effectively read and even kneel in front of chairs and read. The important thing is for the children to choose a spot for themselves, settle in and get to work.

What Do Children Read?

I strongly believe that children should have opportunities to read books that are much too difficult, much too easy and everything in between. As adults, we don't always read the most difficult books when we want to read for pleasure. We choose what I call "Easy Read". Children need opportunities for easy as well as very difficult reading material so they can see where they will be going and growing into.

Should There Be Two Copies of Each Book?

No! Children can share a book and read back and forth to each other from the same book. In a way, it is better to have one book because the children are forced to listen as well as read if they are to understand the content of the story.

Twins

After the reading, each child can complete his/her own synopsis of the story. These can be put on any kind of picture that might match the story. For example, if the children read *The Very Hungry Caterpillar* by Eric Carle, then they could create two caterpillars and write the report on the twin caterpillars. Some full-page formats have been included that are a natural for twin reports such as mittens, tennis shoes and ice-cream cones.

Relax

Teachers have a tendency to be nervous about this type of process because we can't keep our finger on the pace of the classroom and what is being read at every moment. Yes, some children will be mispronouncing some words, and some words will be skipped; however, the children will be highly engaged in the process of reading and doing meaningful, fulfilling activities that are relevant.

Reading Rainbow

This wonderful television show has a segment where children tell about favorite books that they have read. This is a wonderful addition to the buddy reading activities for any classroom. The buddies get to tell about what they read to their peers and then make a recommendation about others reading the same book. The level of comprehension and story details is immediately evident and easy to evaluate using this method.

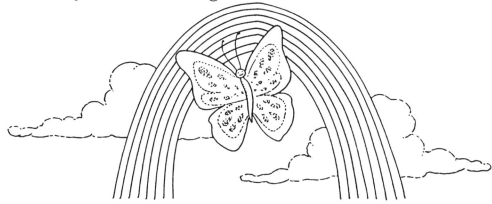

GA1396

_____ read a book to me.

It was fun as fun can be.

Picture from the story.

_____ read a book to me.

It was fun as fun can be.

Picture from the story.

44

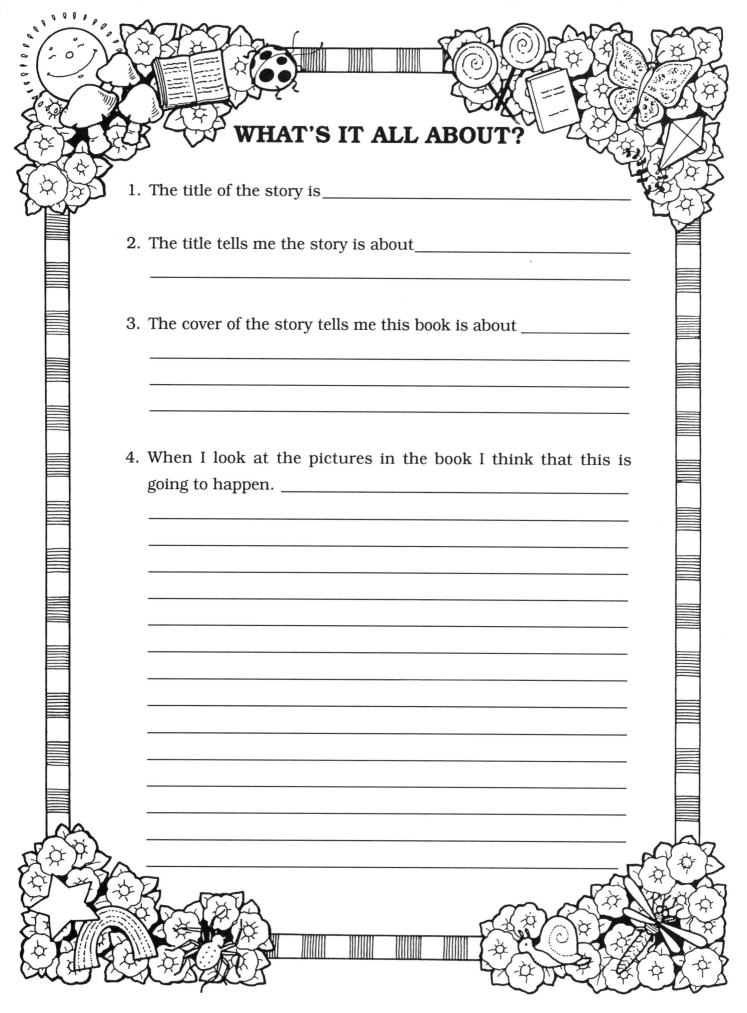

WHAT'S IT ALL ABOUT?

1. The title of the story is _____

2. The title tells me the story is about _____
   _____

3. The cover of the story tells me this book is about _____
   _____
   _____
   _____

4. When I look at the pictures in the book I think that this is
   going to happen. _____
   _____
   _____
   _____
   _____
   _____
   _____
   _____
   _____
   _____
   _____
   _____
   _____
   _____
   _____

Story Title :

READING BUDDIES

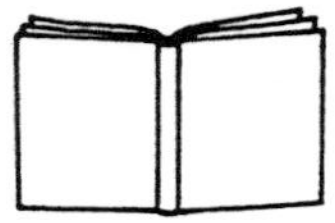

Buddy 1

Beginning of the story

End of the story

New words

Buddy 2

Middle of the story

Main characters

Favorite part

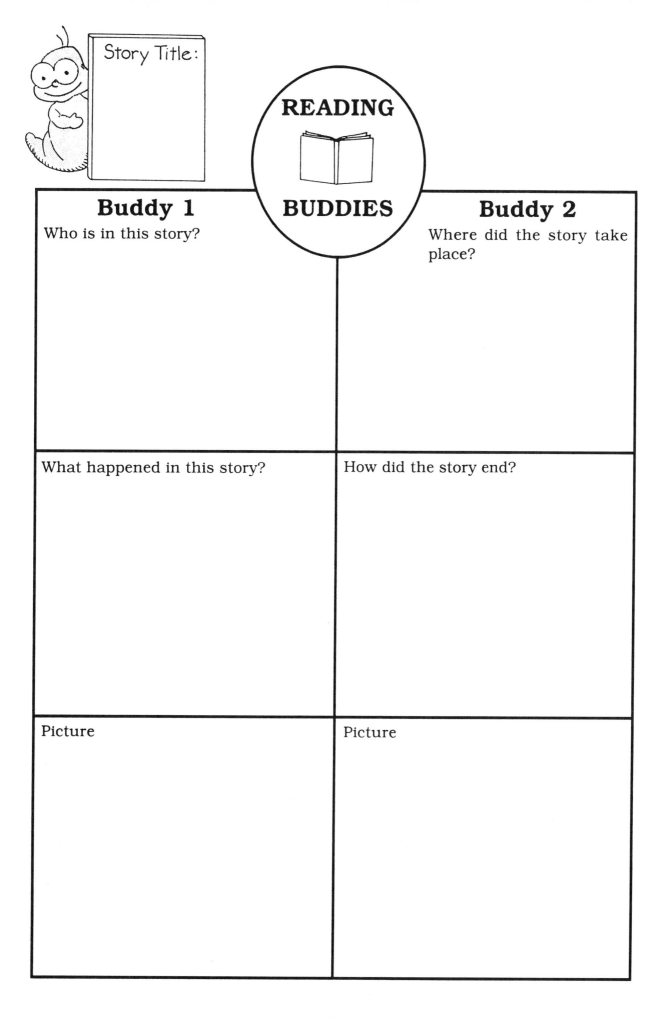

Story Title:

READING

BUDDIES

Buddy 1

Who is in this story?

Buddy 2

Where did the story take place?

What happened in this story?

How did the story end?

Picture

Picture

47

GA1396

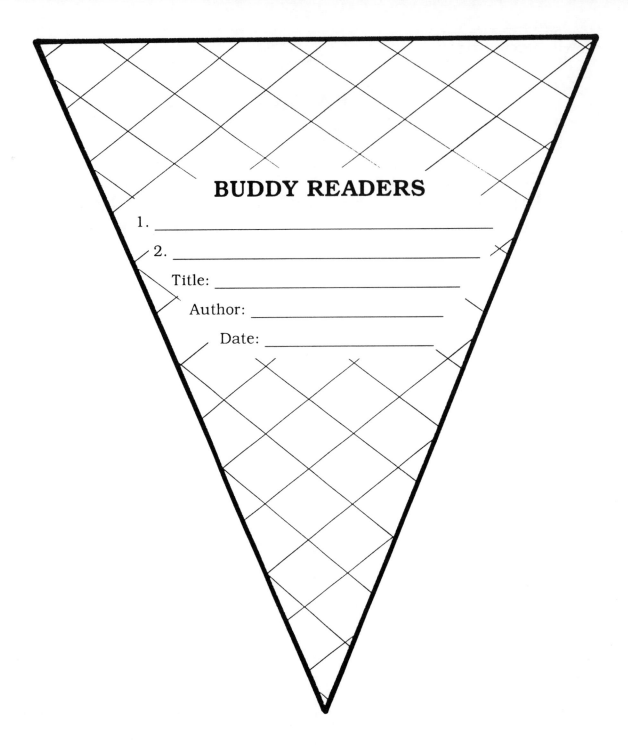

BUDDY READERS

1. _____

2. _____

Title: _____

Author: _____

Date: _____

ICE-CREAM CONE BUDDY READERS

1. Read the story to each other one time/two times. (Teacher circles.)
2. Fill in the ice-cream cone with your names, the title of the book, the author and date.
3. Write about what happened in the story on your ice-cream scoop.
4. Cut out the scoops and ice-cream cone and paste them together.

GA1396

Here's the scoop on what happened in our story.

Here's the scoop on what happened in our story.

MITTEN REPORTS

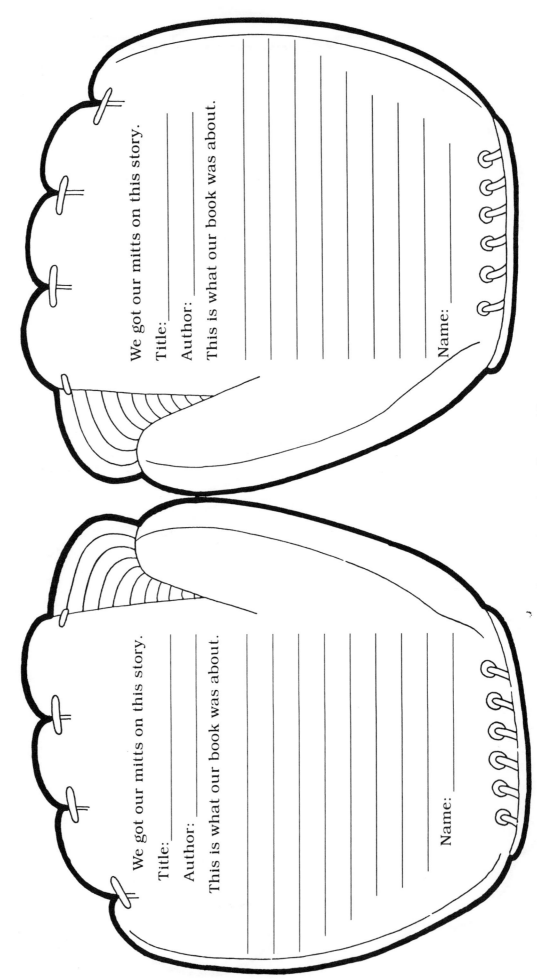

We got our mitts on this story.

Title: _____

Author: _____

This is what our book was about.

_____
_____
_____
_____
_____
_____

Name: _____

We got our mitts on this story.

Title: _____

Author: _____

This is what our book was about.

_____
_____
_____
_____
_____
_____

Name: _____

Tie the mittens together with yarn.

50

GA1396

TENNY TWIN READERS

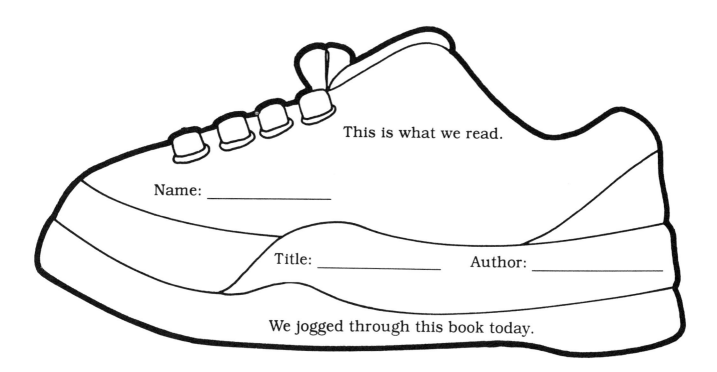

This is what we read.

Name: _____

Title: _____   Author: _____

We jogged through this book today.

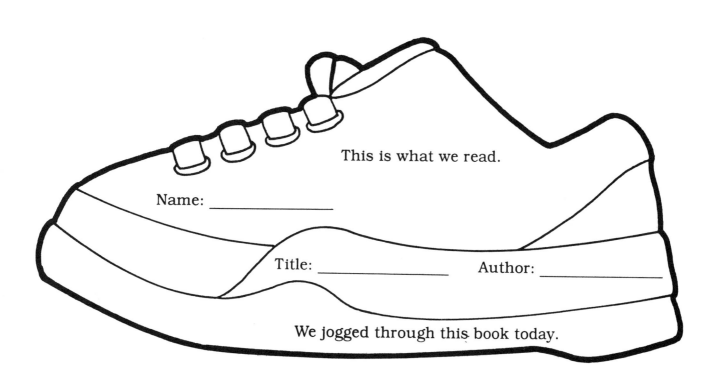

This is what we read.

Name: _____

Title: _____   Author: _____

We jogged through this book today.

GA1396

POETRY AS A TEACHING TOOL

POEMS

Poems are wonderful classroom teaching tools. The children in our classroom keep a poetry notebook, and we add one poem to the notebook every day. Poetry becomes an integral part of our school day.

Poems give children a sense of meter and rhyme. They introduce various ideas and concepts that wouldn't normally be introduced in the classroom. Poetry also offers new and unique vocabulary. A little investigation at the library will quickly give the teacher volumes of good quality poems.

Children love to perform the poems. These quick group activities delight the children and make them avid listeners to each other's interpretations.

Readers' Theatre
Have the children who will be reading come to the front of the room and turn their backs to the audience. As each performer comes to his/her part, the child turns around and faces the audience.

Using Poems to Teach Parts of Speech
Poems provide a natural arena for finding parts of speech. The children are challenged to find the verbs or the adjectives in a sentence. The poems can also be used for vowel and consonant sounds. Poems can be copied on chart paper or put on overheads if copies are not available for the children.

The Scarecrow
This poem lends itself to finding adjectives that describe the scarecrow. The children can list the words that tell about the scarecrow and then do the following activity.

Daytime/Nighttime Scarecrow
Working in pairs, two children can color pictures of the scarecrow by day and by night. Put emphasis on the actions of the scarecrow. The children can wash over pictures with watercolors, using blue for day and black for night. Note: The child doing the night picture should use bright crayons.

Popcorn Evolution
Children enjoy drawing and coloring the different stanzas of the poem. Put them together in groups of four to make a mini mural. Use unpopped and popped popcorn to add to the pictures. Have the children bring in a microwave popcorn bag, a frying pan and a fireplace popcorn popper (if anyone has one). Let the children act out the poem. Finish up the activity with some tasty popcorn and read *The Popcorn Book* by Tomie dePaola.

SCARECROWS

Scarecrows have a funny job.
In cornfields wild with birds,
They chase and shoo to protect the crops
without a single word.

The scarecrow must pretend all day.
He is a mighty force.
Do you suppose when nightfall comes
He snacks on corn? Of course!

S. Rybak

GA1396

POPCORN EVOLUTION

Today I eat my popcorn.
It is easy as can be.
Microwave is the new age.
It's ready one, two, three.

My dad made popcorn on the stove
with oil and salt and butter.
Just three kernels to start out.
They'd pop with such a flutter.

My grandma cooked her popcorn
Upon an open hearth.
In a basket, black with soot,
The popcorn burned and dark.

When Grandma cooked her popcorn
Her nose and cheeks so red,
She ate her popcorn just like me
Before she went to bed.

S. Rybak

IT'S PICTURE DAY, IT'S PICTURE DAY

Today we wear our Sunday best.
I'm wearing my new ruffled dress.

The boys wear ties tied round their necks.
Please take my picture before it wrecks.

Smile and grin and do say, "Cheese."
Stand over there, if you please.

It's time to go and pictures are through.
Hey, don't untie those brand new shoes.

Just wait a minute. Don't mess up your hair.
Put on that tie. Don't give me that glare.

The photographer has some very bad news.
Your pictures must be retaken this afternoon.

S. Rybak

GA1396

IT'S PICTURE DAY, IT'S PICTURE DAY

Draw a picture of the class before school pictures. Don't forget to add these people.

Susan in her red dress
Paul in his blue shirt
David in the green stripes
Mark in the gray sweater
Mary Jane in the blue pants
Kathy with the necklace
Jason in the overalls
Sarah in the pink blouse
Paul with the dirty shirt

Make up one of your own. _____

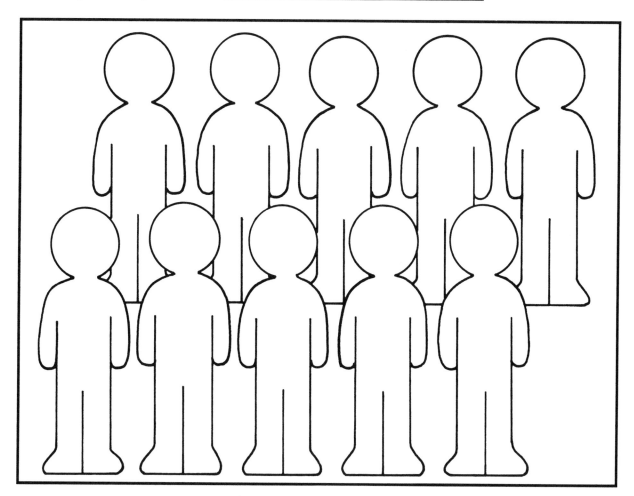

Trade your picture with a partner and see if he/she can find all the special people in the picture. Have him/her write the names and draw arrows to the people once they have been found.

GA1396

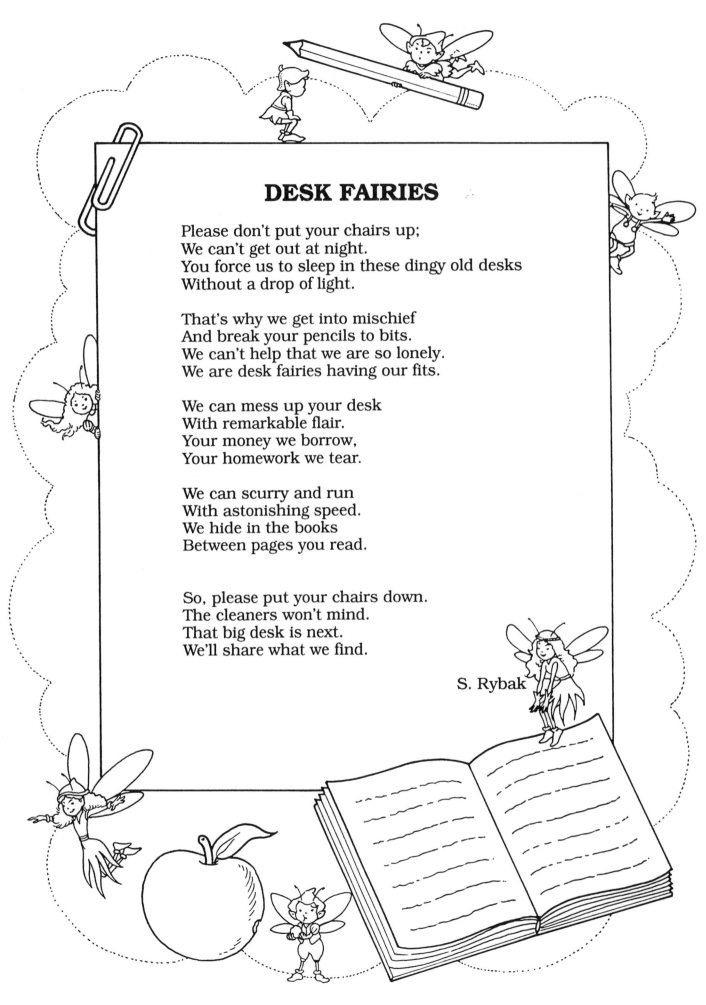

DESK FAIRIES

Please don't put your chairs up;
We can't get out at night.
You force us to sleep in these dingy old desks
Without a drop of light.

That's why we get into mischief
And break your pencils to bits.
We can't help that we are so lonely.
We are desk fairies having our fits.

We can mess up your desk
With remarkable flair.
Your money we borrow,
Your homework we tear.

We can scurry and run
With astonishing speed.
We hide in the books
Between pages you read.

So, please put your chairs down.
The cleaners won't mind.
That big desk is next.
We'll share what we find.

S. Rybak

CREATE A DESK FAIRY FAMILY

Work in groups of three and discuss.

Decide on your fairies' names and ages.

_____   _____

_____   _____

_____   _____

_____   _____

What do they eat, and what do they do for fun?

_____

_____

_____

_____

How did the fairies get here?

_____

_____

_____

_____

What would happen if someone saw one of the fairies?

_____

_____

_____

_____

What kind of mischief do your fairies do?

_____

_____

_____

_____

Each person should draw a picture of a day in the life of a desk fairy. Put them together into a mural.

59

GA1396

SPELLING

Keep Them Posted
Every week I post the spelling words on large chart paper for the children. We use the words in our writing and in our journals. Posting the words gives strong visual reinforcement every time they look up at the chalkboard. This has proven to be very successful when I look at the spelling test scores.

Spelling Partners
Another strategy that goes hand in hand is having the children study their spelling words with partners. This is a daily activity and the children get adjusted to testing each other on the spelling words. Some children will want to say the spellings out loud, and others will need to write the words when they spell them. This is part of each child's learning style which will emerge as they do these activities.

Spelling Checkers
The children usually put their spelling words in alphabetical order every week. I will choose two children who have done this correctly to check all the other papers. They must also check for correct spellings. The children enjoy going to each other for assistance, and the checkers love the responsibility. I will check over the books at a later time to assess their work.

Spelling Units
When the children write, I encourage them to edit their own spelling or to have a buddy read and help them edit the spelling. Even children who can't spell can seem to identify misspelling in someone else's work. This gives a collaborative feeling to the classroom, and the children learn by reading and evaluating someone else's materials.

Kids Choose the Spelling Words
When the children write, I will frequently see a familiar word that keeps reappearing misspelled. I ask the child if he/she would like to have that word on next week's spelling list, and then I add it to the list. Children can also circle words in their writing that they keep misspelling and the teacher can make the list from the class's chosen words. This adds a high degree of motivation because the words were chosen by the children.

Spell-It-Right-When-You-Write Week
This week can reappear throughout the school year. Its purpose is to emphasize to the children the need to apply their spelling skills to their writing. As a class, review the spelling words completed to that time and have groups of children choose words for a spelling review test.

GA1396

WAYS TO HELP CHILDREN COLLABORATE AND SHARE THEIR WRITING USING THE WRITING PROCESS

Together We Write Better

WRITING BUDDIES

Buddy Books
The pattern and instructions for the buddy book on the follow pages make fist-sized books made from one piece of paper. Children love making these books, but it will take some time to teach them all the steps in the process. Once the books are made, the possibilities are endless.

Each book will have eight pages. One suggestion is to let the children read a book and then report on the following details: title, main characters, setting, beginning, middle, ending, best part, least favorite part. These can be written in by the teacher on the master sheet. The children can also write their own stories in these little books and share their masterpieces with their buddies.

Ribbon Stories
These books can be displayed by stapling each of the child's books on a velvet ribbon with a bow at the top. Each child has his/her own ribbon and is motivated to write the stories to see the ribbon stories grow.

Continuing Story
The children can create a continuing story using these little buddy books. Each child can write the beginning of a story and then pass the book on to a neighbor who will finish the story. This allows each child to work on his/her own story, read the other person's story and finish the ending to the partner's story. If page eight and the title page are taped together, the book size and content is doubled.

Diary Writing
These little books also adapt well for mini diaries. These can be written along with a story being read. The children can date the entry and tell about what happened in the story. This is particularly effective with read-aloud chapter books. After a chapter of reading, have the children enter the details they remember into the little diary. These little books can also be shared, and the children can have chapter book discussions in small groups where they may predict what will happen next in the story.

GA1396

BUDDY BOOKS

Step 1:
Fold it the "hot dog" way.

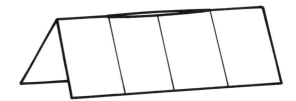

If you did it correctly, the cut will be on the dotted line.

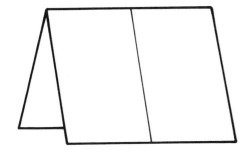

Step 2:
Open it up and fold it the "hamburger" way.

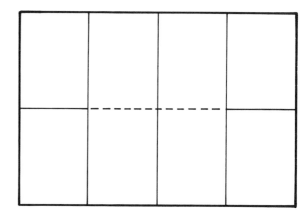

Step 5:
Open your paper and fold it the hot dog way again.

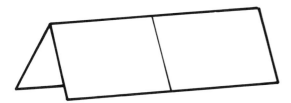

Step 3:
While still folded in the hamburger way, fold it in half again.

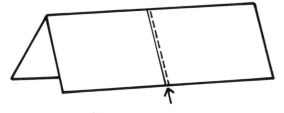

Step 4:
Cut half way up the middle folded line.

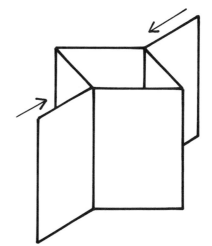

Step 6:
Push the two ends together to create the book.

GA1396

Story Title

1

2

3

The End 8

4

7

5

6

GA1396

STORY WEBS FOR SETTING AND CHARACTER DEVELOPMENT

Setting Web
This web is designed to help children define a specific time and place for their stories. This web can be used so that one child designs the web, and the other child writes the story from the details given. Children can also work together to design the web and then each write his/her own story after deciding on the details. When they are done, they can read each other their stories, edit and share ideas.

The children might enjoy doing this on the overhead projector with the teacher the first few times so they can see the progression of the web. This can be used time and time again when the children are beginning their story development.

Character Web
This web is designed to help children develop details about a character. Each child can develop a character web, and then the children can work together on a story that includes both of the characters. Children can also develop a character web and then share it with another child so they can write the story.

Story Development
After some experience with webs and writing, the children can start with the setting web and move to the character web to develop the beginning of their stories. This will help the children develop stories rich in detail. The children will soon come to recognize how the problem can be developed from the setting and the characters.

Make Your Own Web
The children will begin to enjoy the webbing once they become familiar with the process. The children should be encouraged to create their own webs with partners. Give the children large sheets of paper and help them work through the process of general to specific information gathering.

GA1396

CHARACTER WEB

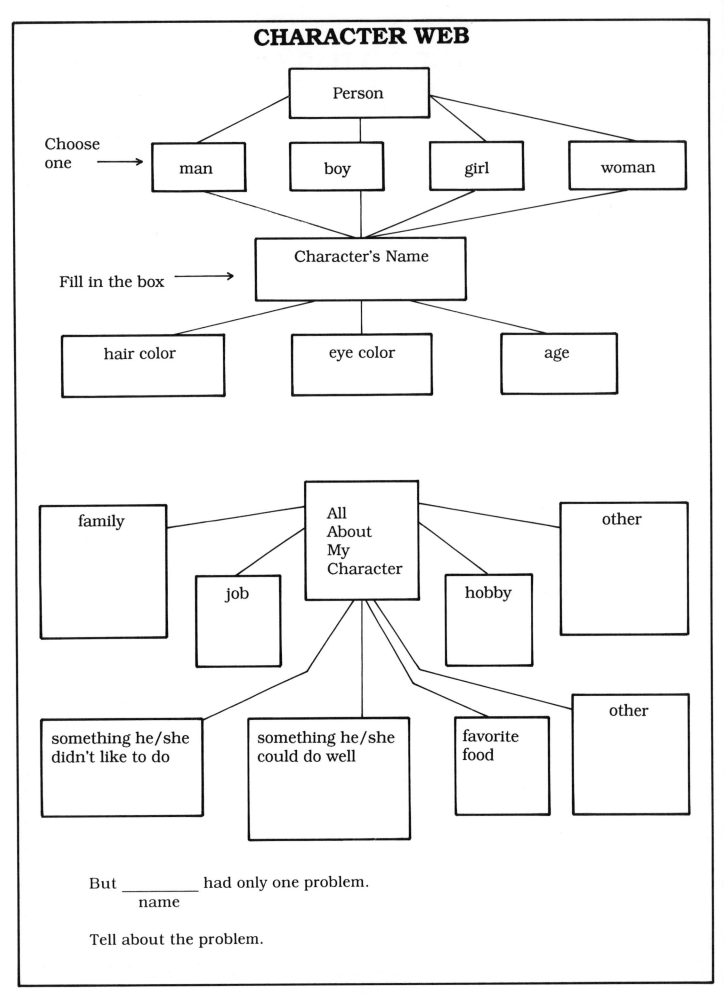

Person

Choose one → man   boy   girl   woman

Fill in the box → Character's Name

hair color   eye color   age

family   All About My Character   other

job   hobby

something he/she didn't like to do   something he/she could do well   favorite food   other

But _____ had only one problem.
          name

Tell about the problem.

Date_____

_____
Story Title

Once upon a time there was a _____ named _____.
man, boy, girl, woman   name

_____'s hair was _____ and his/her eyes were
name   color

_____. _____ was _____ years old.
color   name   age

Here are some interesting things to know about _____.
name

_____

_____

_____

_____

_____

_____

But, _____ had a problem, and this is what it was.
name

_____

_____

_____

_____

_____

_____

_____

_____

_____

_____

_____

_____

GA1396

SETTING WEB

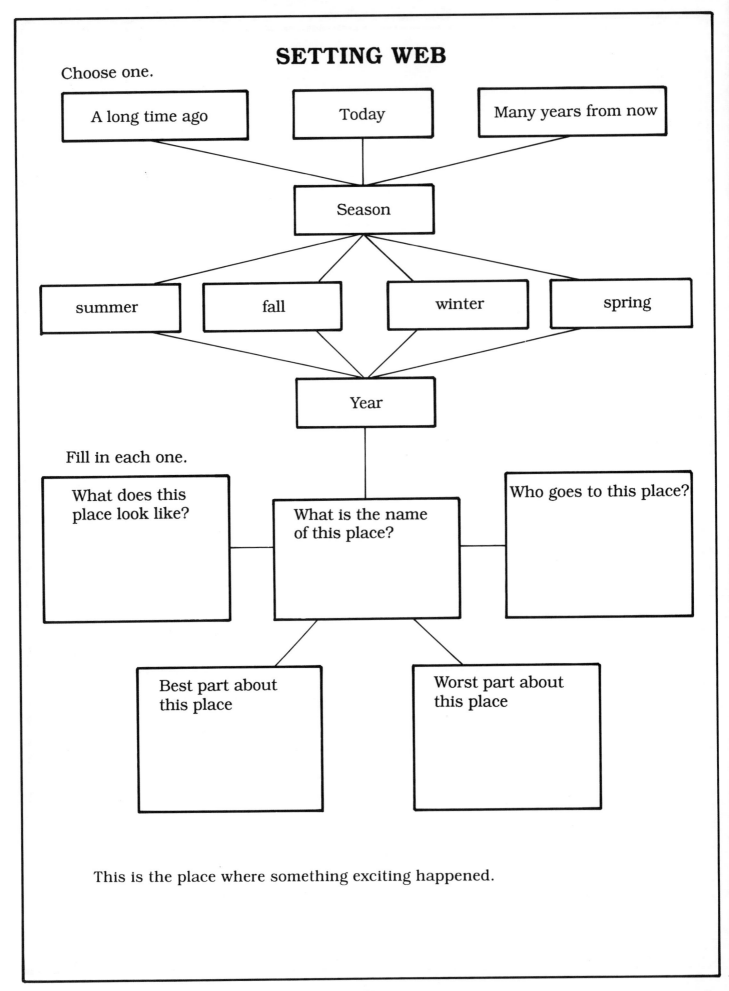

Choose one.

| A long time ago | Today | Many years from now |

Season

summer   fall   winter   spring

Year

Fill in each one.

What does this place look like?

What is the name of this place?

Who goes to this place?

Best part about this place

Worst part about this place

This is the place where something exciting happened.

SPAGHETTI STORIES

Don't you just love something that goes on and on and on and on and on until it's almost silly? These stories remind me of the magician with the scarves up his sleeve that keep coming and coming and coming. Spaghetti stories are sure to create this kind of enthusiasm in your classroom.

Adding Machine Tape

A few rolls of adding machine tape make great beginnings for these stories. One child in the group can start the story, and each individual can add to the drama. It requires each person to read the work that was done previously, and then add his/her own ideas.

Prereaders

This idea can be useful with children who are not yet readers by having each child write a letter of the alphabet and draw a picture. Children can also work on numbers, pictures and simple words.

How to Facilitate the Activity

There are two methods to make this activity work. The first is to have each child measure off the amount of paper needed. Spread the paper on the floor. Let the children work in close proximity so they have to deal with the little bumps and wiggles. This is bound to cause little disturbances and space violations, but this is not all bad. Once children see this process as a group product and get past working near other individuals, they will begin to enjoy the process and the finished product.

The second way to facilitate this with children is to let each child write his/her ideas and then hand the work to the next individual. This could be an activity that would need to be completed at the end of a day so each child could make a contribution throughout the day. Each team should have an opportunity to read their story to the class. Display the stories by hanging them from the lights or ceiling like streamers.

GA1396

SPAGHETTI STORIES FOR SEQUENCING

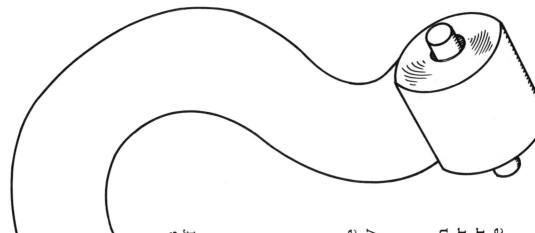

This method of group writing is certainly popular with children and is a tremendous asset when teaching time lines and sequencing. Children understand the concept of order and can learn to put simple events in a sequence. Here are some suggestions.

Getting up in the morning
The school day
Brushing your teeth
Building a birdhouse
Walking the dog
Buying groceries

It is amazing how many steps the children will eliminate. A group can be responsible for figuring out the steps and then illustrating them in sequence. Other groups may want to comment on steps that are missing or out of order.

Fairy Tales on Computer Paper
Computer paper is another great resource for these types of activities. Children can work in groups and try to retell a familiar fairy tale together. This takes some teacher direction with young children, but older children can work independently. Together they must decide on the parts they will illustrate and the text they will write. The stories can be hung like banners across the room.

GA1396

LET'S EDIT

Children can assist each other and can learn from each other in the process of editing each other's material. This can be done in a variety of ways.

Read to Me

Children can simply read each other their stories and ask them if it makes sense. In the process of reading, the children will see and hear their own errors and be able to make changes.

Let Me See

Children can read each other's work and point out simple errors such as punctuation and capitalization. Children may not have punctuation in their own work but can easily find someone else's errors.

Teacher Note About Writing

Young children cannot be expected to write using proper punctuation when they are in the beginning stages of the writing process. Writing requires the child's attention to the content and details of the story. The child will be creative and be searching for words. The conventions involving punctuation are not mastered by the child, so these must be thought of separately. This is an entirely different process. The editing process is an essential step in the writing process. It allows children the opportunity to go back to their work and look at it with a new perspective.

Not Everything Needs an Edit

When children do a great deal of writing, it is unrealistic to think that everything is going to get edited or that it needs an edit. As adults, we quickly jot down notes or write messages and don't bother to edit; however, with more formal letters and business correspondence, we take the time to edit. Children need the same freedom. Writing should always be realistic to the way we use the written language in our environment.

GA1396

CLASS BOOK
EXTENSIONS

GA1396

CLASS BOOKS

Books shared in a classroom become part of the class culture. Favorite books or poems that are read and reread continue to be shared by the children on the playground and at home. A great way to share a book in a classroom is to create a class book. These class books are usually an extension or a takeoff on an idea presented in the book. The books allow for higher level thinking skills and creative interpretation. The children experience a cooperative belonging in contributing to the final product.

The book extensions on the following pages are some of my personal favorites and favorites of the children I teach. Each is designed to be used in a different way. Some of the activities call for one class book, and others can be done in small groups. Any of these books can also be done by individual children.

A Note About Book Binding

Our school has purchased a spiral book binding machine that puts a plastic binding on the ends of our books. This is the ideal binding for young authors' manuscripts. These books can also be put together with the lacing method of hole punch and yarn lacing. Curling ribbon is also very sturdy and attractive on the children's work.

Many Lucious Lollipops by Ruth Heller

This delightful book by Ruth Heller focuses on explaining adjectives to children. Ms. Heller is known for her beautiful, vivid illustrations that complement the text. Extensions on this book give children firsthand experience identifying and using adjectives.

The cover for the children's book is a giant lollipop. The children's pages are blank paper in the shape of a lollipop without the stick. A flat edge is left for binding the book together. If the cover is run off on tagboard, a Popsicle stick can be taped to the back and used as the stick.

Children are to think of favorite foods and use adjectives to describe the foods and illustrate their ideas. This can also be extended into other books about animals, transportation or any other category.

Lollipop Art

Giant lollipops can be hung from the ceiling to celebrate this activity. The children can color or paint giant lollipops on tagboard. Cut the circles out and mount a giant stick on the bottom. Cover the lollipops with bright colored cellophane and tie them with curling ribbon.

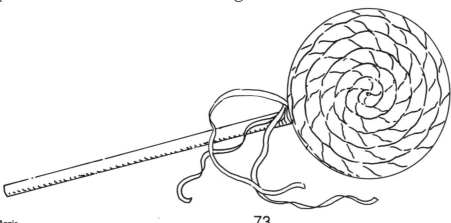

GA1396

Lollipops are lovely, sticky, licky and tasty.

The children will each pick a different food and use adjectives to describe the food. For example, spaghetti is stringy, spicy, long, messy and fun.

Read *Many Lucious Lollipops* by Ruth Heller.

74

GA1396

Leo the Late Bloomer by Robert Kraus

In this story, Leo the Tiger can't grow up. He can't read or write or eat neatly. His parents are worried, especially Leo's father. Children like Leo's triumphant success at the end of this book, and teachers enjoy sharing the fact that there was no cure other than time to develop and grow.

Children have landmarks that tell them when they have bloomed. A class discussion following the reading of this book brings out some interesting activities that children see as having bloomed. Here are a few of my favorites.

When I bloom I'll be able to

> sleep all night at my friend's house
> ride my bike around the block
> read
> sleep on the top bunk

Children have goals and aspirations, and this book does a delightful job of helping children get a step closer to reaching their goals.

Blooming Flowerpots

The flowerpots can be created by each child and bound into a class book. The teacher can also create a bulletin board with a giant flowerpot or window box. The children can make giant flowers and write their "blooming activities" on the stems of the flowers.

When
I
Bloom

I'll be able to

Read *Leo the Late Bloomer*
by Robert Kraus.

GA1396

Cloudy with a Chance of Meatballs by Judi Barrett

I have never read this book and had children who haven't giggled, moaned and stared in wonder at the pictures. Food that falls regularly from the sky is a wonderful idea until the storms and oversized food hit the town of Chewandswallow.

The book cover is a giant piece of bread. Each child gets a piece of paper in the shape of a slice of bread and creates something that is made from giant food. The children can also cut food pictures from magazines and create their pictures using these materials.

Critical Thinking for the Folks of Chewandswallow

1. What problems might you have if it rained food every day?

2. The weather turned bad and delivered horrible combinations of food. List other horrible food combinations.

3. The people of Chewandswallow chose to leave in order to solve their problem. List many different and unusual ways they could have solved their problem.

4. Decide if the townspeople made the right decision to leave the town of Chewandswallow.

5. Go back to the town of Chewandswallow and tell what it looks like today.

Kites Sail High by Ruth Heller

This book puts the focus on verbs. The beautiful illustrations and easy to understand text help children understand the concept of the verb, but in order for children to truly understand, they must DO. This little book gives the early learner a great opportunity. Each child chooses an animal and then writes a sentence that starts like this: Elephants can....This gives the children a clear shot at finding verbs rather than adjectives. Other helping verbs can also be used in place of the word *can.*

Cut blank pages that match the cover, one for each of the children. They can focus on their favorite animals and find verbs that describe the animals' actions. Older children may want to do their own books or do one with a partner.

GA1396

Read *Cloudy with a Chance of Meatballs* by Judy Barrett.

**Look What
We Could Make
with
Giant Food**

Each child will make a different item with various giant foods. For example, use donuts for wheels, a candy bar for the car body and licorice for the road.

Children can also cut pictures of food from magazines for details.

GA1396

Each child will pick a different critter and write a sentence to match the animal's actions. All sentences should start with the animal name and the word *can*. For example: Butterflies can fly, flap, flutter, swoop and rest.

Read Kites Sail High by Ruth Heller.

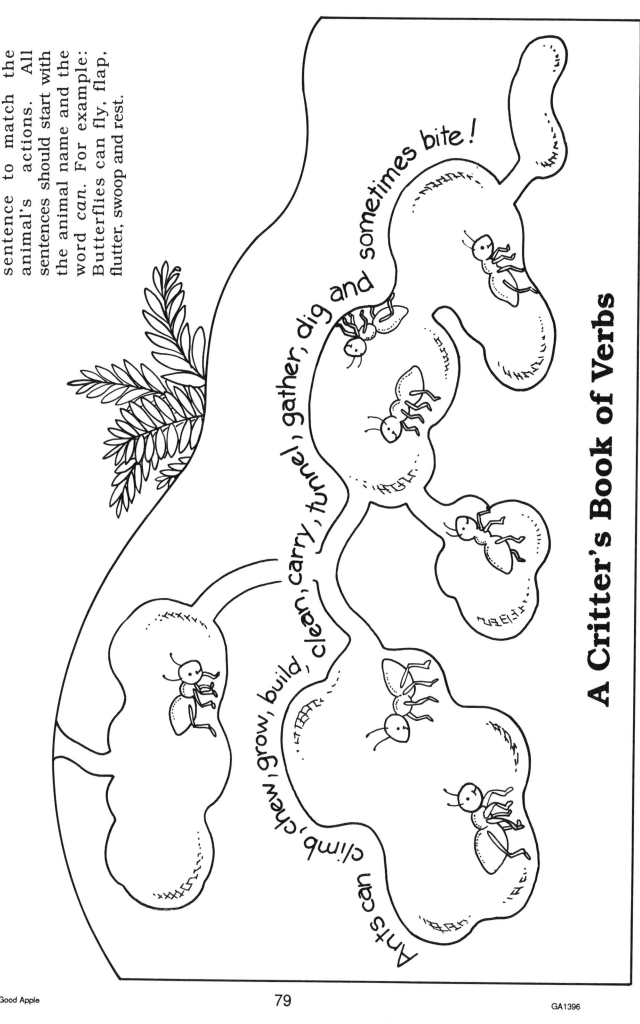

Ants can climb, chew, grow, build, clean, carry, tunnel, gather, dig and sometimes bite!

A Critter's Book of Verbs

79

Read *It Looked Like Spilt Milk* by Charles G. Shaw.

The fun part to this book is that no two pages have the same shape. Each child gets a piece of interfacing. This is a white stiff material used to line suits. It can be purchased inexpensively at a fabric store. This material is very tough and can take lots of abuse but still cuts quite easily. The children can design their cloud creations and color the material. Interfacing is very receptive to markers and crayons. Punch a hole at the top of each cloud and tie the pages together with the ribbon.

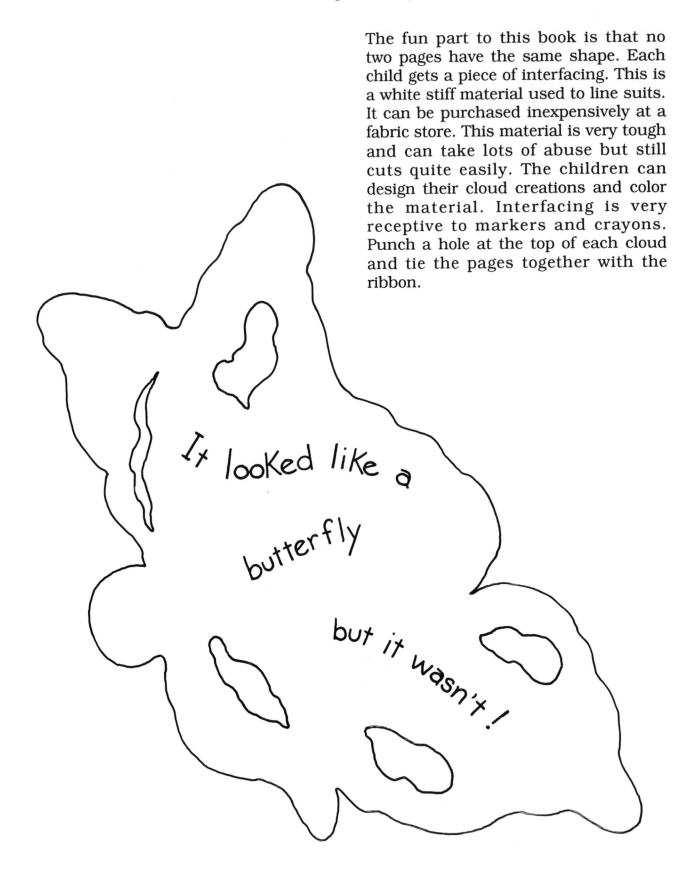

It looked like a butterfly but it wasn't!

GA1396

Read *Frederick* by Leo Lionni.

A Class Diorama

The children make field mice from thistles gathered in the fall. Little eyes, ears and tails can be added. Use craft glue to insure that the details will stay in place. Adult supervised glue guns also work well. After the children make their mice, they can put them into a class diorama. In a quick trip around the school grounds, the children can gather small sticks, leaves, rocks and any other ground covering that would make a nest for the little mice. The nest can be created in a large box, and then the children can arrange their mice in the correct positions.

81

GA1396

The Jolly Postman or Other People's Letters
by Janet and Allan Ahlberg

This is, without a doubt, my favorite book of all time. The story is about a little postman who delivers letters to various fairy tale characters. Envelopes and little letters are included with stamps and postmarks. My children loved this book so much, I had to think of a way to turn it into a book extension. The following activity can be done with a small group of five children each doing one of the character letters. Children can also create their own books and share their stories with the class. Either way, this is sure to be a good learning experience and great fun.

The Postman's Story
The postman in the story can take on a variety of fun characteristics. My children wrote about the silly postman who was always getting lost or the awesome postman who saved the day. Children can use any adjective they choose to describe their postmen and adventures.

To Assemble the Book
The book should have a cover made of tagboard, and the inside pages should alternate between a blank page for the postman's story and an envelope. Use tagboard on the back of the book. Inexpensive envelopes can be used, or the children can make their own from the page that is provided.

Creating Addresses for the Characters
Inside everyone's address is the essence of his/her community. After the individual's name comes his/her house number, and after the number, the street on which he/she lives. Next comes the city that he/she lives in, and finally, the state. Don't forget the ZIP code.

This book gives the children a chance to experiment with their community and match it with the story details.

Postage Stamps
The children can design their own postage stamps after studying a few examples. Packages of beginning stamp collector kits can also produce a large variety of colorful and inexpensive stamps for the children to use.

Postmarks
This book also gives children an opportunity to take a closer look at the marks put on mail by the postal service. Children can learn where the letter came from and the day and time it was mailed by close examination of the postmark.

GA1396

ENVELOPE PATTERN

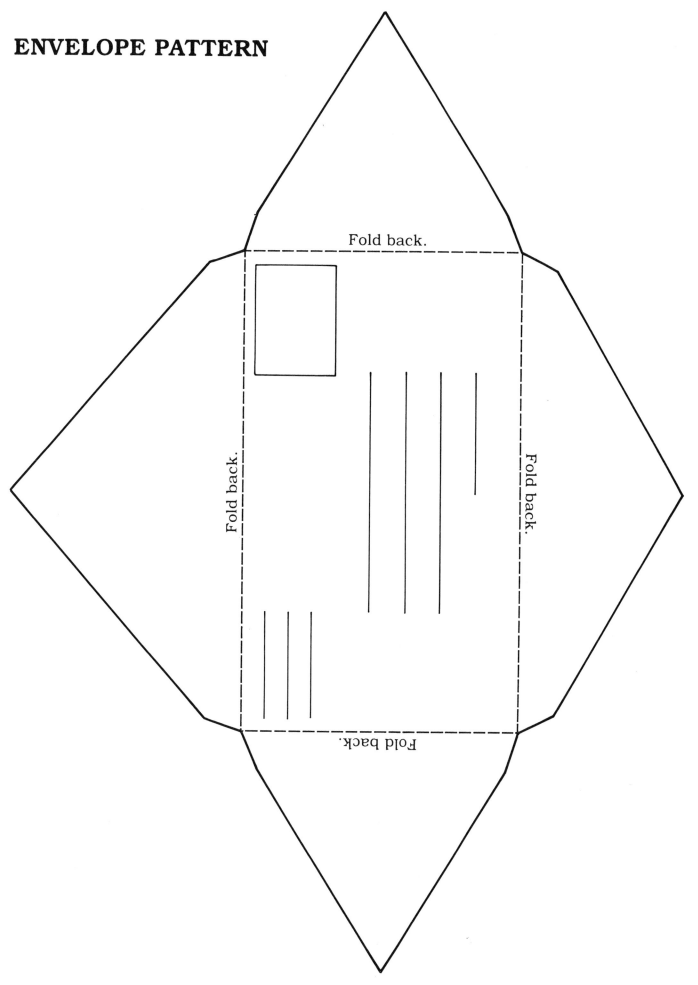

Fold back.

Fold back.

Fold back.

Fold back.

83

GA1396

BILLS FROM THE MALL FOR THE EMPEROR'S NEW CLOTHES

The poor emperor was so embarrassed after he walked around town in his underwear that he decided to do some shopping at the mall to get some nice new clothes. When the emperor got his bill, he couldn't believe his eyes.

- What day did the emperor do his shopping?
- What are the names of the stores where the emperor shopped?
- What did the emperor buy at the store?
- How much did the emperor spend altogether?
- How much did the emperor pay toward his bill?

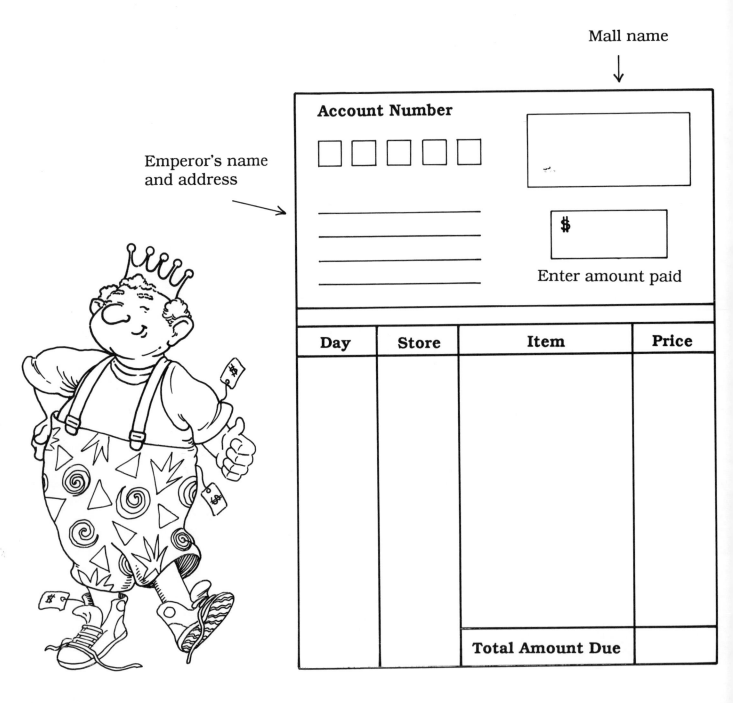

Mall name

Account Number

Emperor's name and address

$

Enter amount paid

Day	Store	Item	Price
		Total Amount Due	

GA1396

LITTLE RED RIDING HOOD
MAKES A WRONG TURN

On the front of the postcard, draw a picture of the place Little Red Riding Hood went instead of going to Granny's house.

Little Red Riding Hood made a wrong turn. Design a postcard that tells where she went and what she had to say about her vacation.

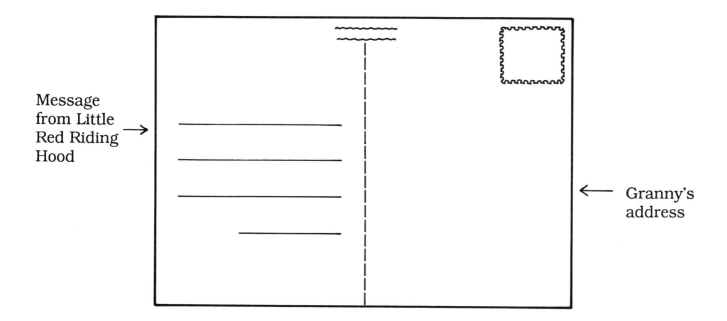

Message from Little Red Riding Hood →

← Granny's address

85

GA1396

MATTRESS ADVERTISEMENT
FOR THE PRINCESS AND THE PEA

In the story "The Princess and the Pea," the princess had some difficulty sleeping through the night. She could feel the nasty little pea under all the mattresses set up by the queen's helpers.

Pretend that the princess receives an advertisement for a mattress sale. Ask yourself these questions.

- What would the princess want the mattress to do?
- What is the mattress filled with? How much does the mattress cost?
- What is the name of the mattress store?
- Where is this store?
- What is the phone number?

Next, design the advertisement for the mattress store. Put the princess' address on the outside of the envelope. Put the return address of the mattress store in the correct location. Cut out your advertisement and put it into the envelope.

SPECIAL SALE!
EVERYTHING MUST GO!

PRINCESS SAVINGS

SPECIAL PRICE

Phone number:

_____

Look for our new store at:

_____

_____

_____

We accept

GA1396

THANK-YOU NOTES FROM THE COUNTRY MOUSE AND THE CITY MOUSE

The City Mouse thought that the country was terrible. He didn't like the food and thought that life was pretty boring for the Country Mouse. The Country Mouse didn't like the city. He thought that the city was dangerous and much too busy. Each mouse wrote a thank-you note to the other to say thanks for the vacation, but no thanks. Write a letter from the City or Country Mouse and tell how you felt about your vacation. Don't forget to be polite. Even though they do not like where each lives, they are still friends.

1. Design a cover on this half of the thank-you note.
2. Cut out your thank-you note and fold it in half on the dotted line.
3. On the inside, write your message to the Country Mouse or the City Mouse.

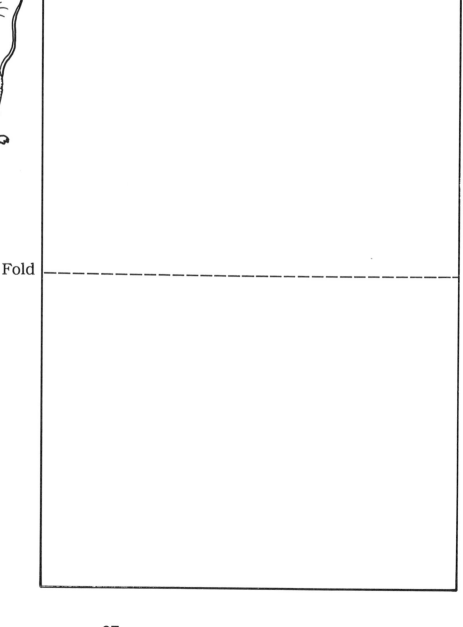

Fold

87

GOLDILOCKS GETS AN INVITATION FROM THE THREE BEARS

The Three Bears are glad that Goldilocks is now older and knows better than to break into bear homes. After the break-in, they had a long talk with Goldilocks' mother, and the two families became friends. The Three Bears are going to have a little party for Goldilocks' birthday.

- How old will Goldilocks be on her birthday?
- What will they have to eat at the party?
- Where will the party be held?
- What time will the party begin?
- If Goldilocks is coming, she should call the bears to let them know. What is the bears' phone number?

Fold

On the inside, write the message. Think about the questions and include the answers in your invitation.

Decorate the front of the birthday party invitation.

Cut out the card and fold on the dotted line.

Address your envelope to Goldilocks with a return address for the Three Bears.

GA1396

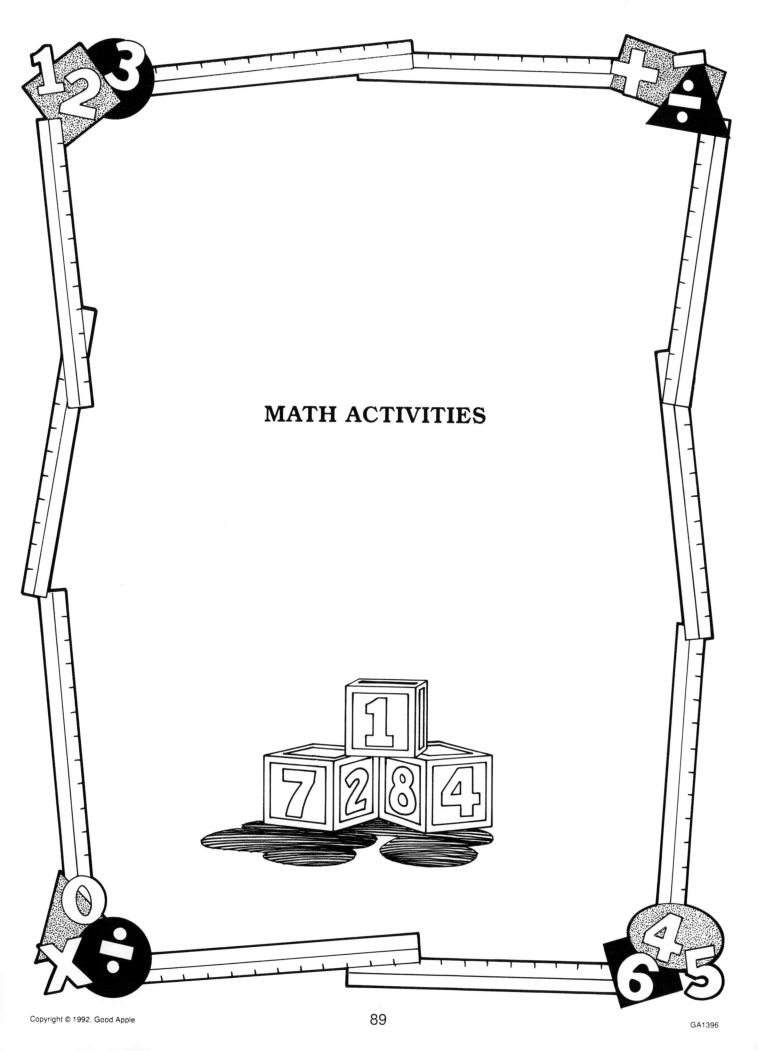

MATH ACTIVITIES

GA1396

Math activities can be one of the most natural cooperative learning experiences. Young children need opportunities to work with objects to establish a concrete understanding of relationships. Children also need to have many math experiences beyond number recognition. The activities that are listed give children opportunities to experience math using manipulatives that assist the group and make the concept relevant.

Your Piece Is Bigger Than My Piece

Children are forever fighting with each other over the size of cake pieces. "His piece is bigger than my piece." Everyone wants the biggest piece.

The cookie page is a simple version of division problems that would be appropriate to use with young children. It could also be used as an introduction to the cake page. On the cookie page, the children can cut out their cookies and put them on the rack to cool. With young children, keep the groups to two or four children. By changing the number of children of either activity, the process will become more complex. Three children will have a difficult time dividing eight cookies.

In this activity, each group of four children is given the cake page. Give only one page per group. The children must divide the cake so that everyone gets the same amount. Keep the children away from scissors until they have had time to discuss their strategy for dividing the cake.

How Big Is a Giant Step?

If Susan and Mary work together, they can decide exactly how big a giant step really is. They can even name it the "Marsan" after themselves. After the teams have determined how large their giant step should be, they can cut out a giant footstep. Rolls of white paper or brown wrapping paper can be used. Have the children follow the directions for creating the footstep. Let the children make their own footsteps. This will aid the measuring process.

The activity page will give the children their initial exploration into a giant measurement. The children should be taught that one giant puts down its footstep, and then the next footstep is butted up against the first.

After the children are done, have them compare their measurements with other teams. Did they need more footsteps to cover the same area? Why? Did the width of the footsteps change the number of the measurement?

COOKIE CUTTERS

Pass out the cookies. Make sure everyone in your group gets the same amount of cookies.

COOKIES ON THE COOLING RACK

1

2

3

4

GA1396

CUT THE CAKES

Cut the cakes. Make sure everyone in your group gets the same amount.

GIANT FOOTSTEPS

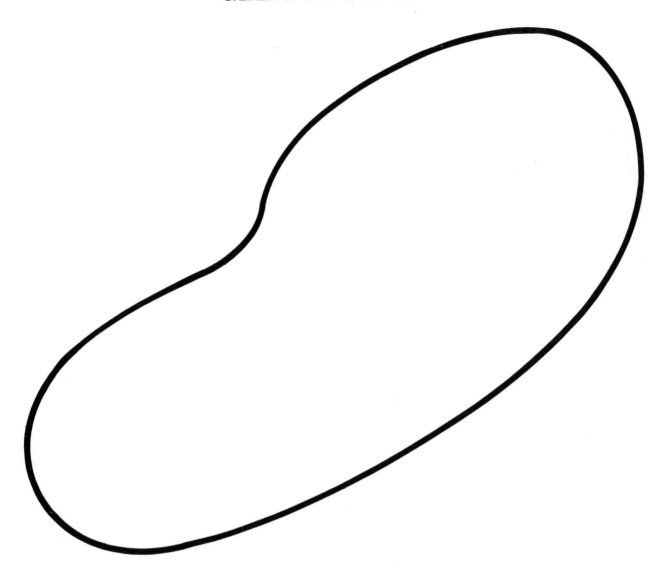

1. How many giant footsteps to the door? _____

2. How many giant footsteps to the bathroom? _____

3. How many giant footsteps to the office? _____

4. How many giant footsteps to the playground? _____

5. How many giant footsteps to _____? _____
Fill in your own.

6. How many giant footsteps did you take altogether? _____

GA1396

THE BOSSY BLUE JAY

This activity allows the children to sort, pattern and weigh using bird seeds. The teacher will need to provide small bags and about two ounces of seeds for each child. The seeds should be a mixture of at least three different types. Seeds are an inexpensive commodity that can be used repeatedly for math activities.

The first activity has the children sorting the seeds into three groups by size. In the second activity, the children pattern the seeds using three different types of seeds. This would be an ABC pattern. In the final activity, the children weigh the seeds on a small postal scale. This will mix the seeds back together. Weigh the seeds in a small medicine vial or a small plastic bag.

Interesting seed activities can be started with these three pages. Let the children explore various seeds that are used for a variety of purposes. Children should also see the seed in its own environment and separate from the plant it comes from. Pet store seeds, peanuts, popcorn and spices such as mustard and fennel seeds are just a few of the seeds that are available for exploration. Avocado plants can be started from the seed. Children also enjoy finding seeds in a banana. Children are quick to recognize that big plants don't always have the biggest seeds.

Small rodents are attracted to seeds in the cold winter months so keep the seeds in an airtight container when not in use.

Don't forget to plant some of the seeds to see if they will grow. Most seeds need to dry naturally and will rot if planted directly from the original plant. For insured success, use seeds from seed packets.

THE FORGOTTEN SEEDS

When blue jay, sparrow and squirrel measured their seeds, a few fell to the ground and grew. Have the children plant some sunflower seeds and some grass seeds. Have them estimate which seed will sprout first and which will eventually grow the largest.

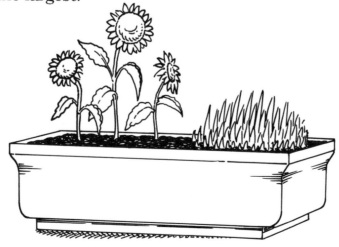

GA1396

THE BOSSY BLUE JAY

Once upon a time, there was a blue jay. He was a bossy little blue jay. He liked to tease the squirrels and chase the little sparrows. The blue jay was greedy and loved to eat the biggest and fattest seeds. He wanted all the good seeds for himself.

The squirrel also loved the fat meaty seeds and so did the sparrow. The blue jay decided that the only solution was to sort the seeds into groups so that each animal would get his own seeds and nobody would have to share. Of course, the blue jay decided that he should get the sunflower seeds because they are the biggest and fattest seeds. The other animals could choose their seeds, but nobody could have the large sunflower seeds.

Help the animals sort the seeds in the flowers below. Give the blue jay the largest seeds, the squirrel the next largest seeds and the sparrow the smallest seeds.

GA1396

The squirrel and the sparrow did not like this idea one little bit. They missed having different types of seeds to eat, and they didn't think it was very fair. The animals had a meeting and decided that the only good way to fix this problem was for all of them to take turns eating all the different seeds. That night, the animals worked in groups of three and put the seeds in order so everyone could eat his fair share.

Pattern the seeds to make rows of big seeds, middle-sized seeds and small seeds.

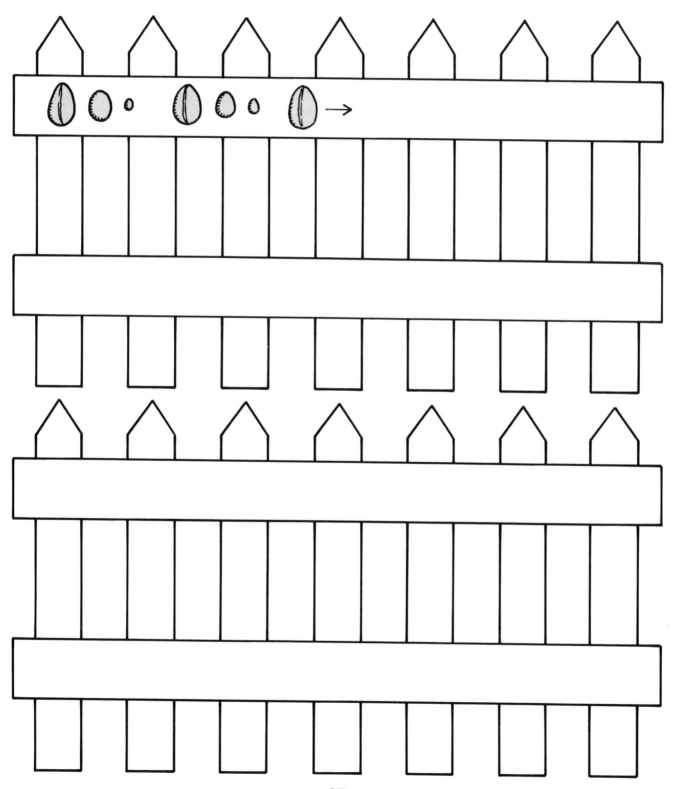

GA1396

The blue jay got very angry with this idea and decided that the only fair way to settle this problem was to weigh the seeds and give each animal his fair amount of food. The blue jay decided that the sparrow should get one ounce of seeds and that the squirrel should get two ounces, but the bluejay thought he should get three ounces because it was his idea. The birds measured the seeds and put them away in storage until they could eat them.

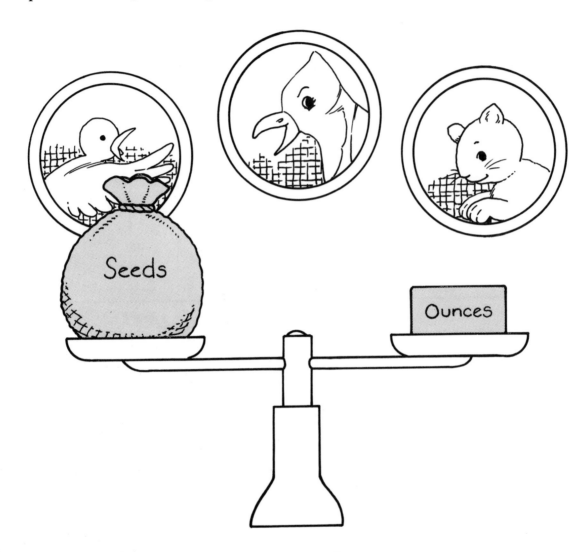

How many sunflower seeds are in one ounce?

Estimate: _____

Actual Number: _____

If you were one of the animals, what way would you sort the seeds so that everyone got a fair share? _____

_____

_____

GA1396

TEAM TIME TELLING

Two children can easily practice telling time with this simple activity. Each team will need to make one clock, but the children may each want to make one of their own. One person tells the time, and the other person sets the clock to the correct time. A digital clock and clock with hands have both been provided. Duplicate the clocks on heavier card stock paper to make them last.

When the children are ready, they can do the activity in a variety of ways. One can set the clock and the other has to write down the time. One child can call out a time and the other can set the clock. To increase the difficulty, one child can state a time and the other child has to set the clock ahead by thirty minutes.

M & M's Estimation

In this activity the children totally explore a small bag of M & M's candy. Start the activity by showing the children the large bag that holds the small bags of candy. Have the children estimate the cost of the large bag. After they are done with the estimation, show them the actual cost. As a class, discuss the differences. Next, have the children estimate the total number of small bags in the big bag. Count out the actual number and compare the difference.

The children should then estimate the number of M & M's in their bags of candy. Will each bag have the same number of candy or will it be different? Next, the children should estimate the number of reds, yellows, greens, light browns, oranges and dark browns. After the children are done with their estimations, they should count the number of candies and then graph their results.

When the children work on this activity, each one should have his/her own bag of candy and paper but should be working next to another child. This allows the children the opportunity to compare their experience to another's and gives them a point of reference.

Finally, after all the data has been collected, let the children eat the M & M's (this is the best part). Make a class graph of the total number of each color as a culminating activity.

GA1396

DIGITAL TEAM TIME

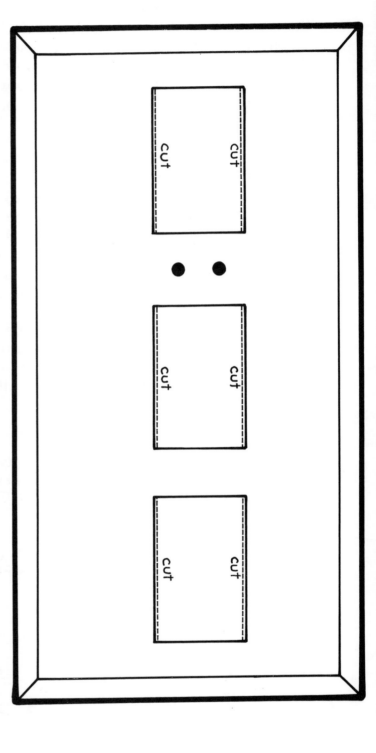

GA1396

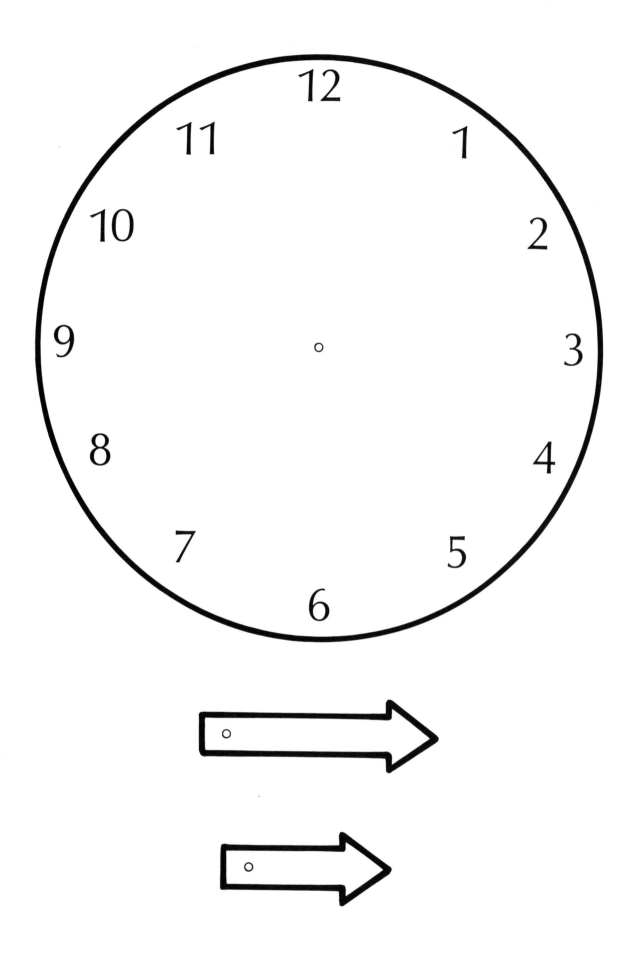

101

M & M'S ESTIMATION

1. What is the cost of the big bag of M & M's?

_____   _____
        Estimation   Actual cost

2. How many small bags of M & M's are in the big bag?

_____   _____
        Estimation   Actual number

3. Will each bag have the same number of candies?

_____   _____
            Yes   No

4. How many M & M's are in your small bag?

_____   _____
        Estimation   Actual number

5. How many candies of each color are in the bag?

red   _____   _____

yellow   _____   _____

green   _____   _____

light brown _____   _____

dark brown _____   _____

orange   _____   _____
                   Estimation   Actual number

GA1396

M & M GRAPH

Numbers	red	yellow	green	light brown	dark brown	orange
10						
9						
8						
7						
6						
5						
4						
3						
2						
1						

103

GA1396

SCIENCE ACTIVITIES

GA1396

Science provides a natural environment for children to have fun and explore in groups of two or more. Because of the hands-on nature of science, it may be best to keep the groups to the smallest number possible so everyone will get an adequate amount of exploration time.

FLOATING FRIENDS

Materials that sink and float are a recurring theme in the primary grades. Young children enjoy the water play and are always surprised by some of the materials that refuse to sink.

This lab experience has the children working in teams of two or three. Their mission is to get a sinking object to float. They may use only the materials that are given. The teacher can put together trays of materials that the children will use.

The following work sheet indicates that the children will need a piece of paper, a paper clip, a small ball of clay (use the clay from art class and not play dough) and a small rock. The children can make a small boat from the paper or the clay and the paper clip will float inside.

On the activity sheet, the children are to keep track of their different trials and then write about the one that worked best.

MAKE A MAGNET RACE

Children love magnetism. In this activity, the children make their own magnets from existing magnets. A steel nail that is fairly flat on the end is required. I use large nails that the children can grasp and fairly large school magnets.

The children all start at the same time. They rub the magnet over the nail in the same direction from top to bottom. They continue doing this until they think it is ready to attract a paper clip. The first person who can attract a paper clip to his/her nail is the winner.

The children actually need to rub about 100 to 150 strokes to create a magnet. The restructured electrons will eventually return to normal.

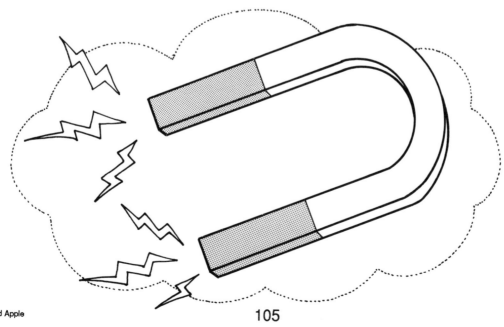

GA1396

EXPLORE THE MYSTERY OBJECT

Much of science is the art of observation. It is important for the children to have the opportunity to explore something they know little to nothing about. This activity allows the children to work together as detectives to find clues about the mystery object.

The mystery object might be an old-fashioned egg beater, a computer tape or a stamp dispenser. The kitchen will often provide unusual objects that do specific jobs. The children need to explore the object and describe it with words that tell how it feels, looks, what it is used for and how it works. The children then give the object a name and draw a picture of someone using the object.

After everyone has had a turn with the object, have the class discuss what each group thought the object was. Give the awards to the groups that came the closest to guessing the object's correct use and an award for the most creative answers.

The fun part about this activity is that it can go on all year long. A different object can be put into the mystery box and the children can explore a variety of mysterious objects as partners all year long.

FOOD CHAIN GAME

In this activity, the children will make their own gameboard and learn to play a simple game that instructs them about the concepts of *predator* and *prey*. The food chain for this gameboard starts with the leaf and moves to an aphid. The ladybug is next, followed by the spider. The spider is followed by the bird and the bird by the cat.

Four children color and cut out the gameboard pieces. When all four pieces are assembled, they can be mounted together on a piece of tagboard. The children then use glue and sand or cornmeal to give texture to the web and leave it to dry overnight.

Each of the four players takes a playing piece. The only four game pieces are the aphid, the ladybug, the spider and the bird. The leaves and the cat are not game pieces because the leaf does not have a prey and the cat does not have a predator. After some playing time, the children may question this. Give them time to draw their own answers.

The rules to this game are quite simple. The first child will role a single die. If you land on a critter that will eat you (your predator), you lose a turn. If you land on a critter that you will eat (your prey), then you take an extra turn. Two to four people can play at one time, and the first person to get to the center of the web wins the game.

The Grouchy Ladybug and *The Very Busy Spider* by Eric Carle are both excellent resources for these activities.

GA1396

CAN YOU GET IT TO FLOAT?

Rules: Using a piece of paper, a paper clip, a small ball of clay, a small rock get the paper clip to float on top of the water.

Trial #1

What did you do?

How did it work?

Trial #2

What did you do?

How did it work?

Trial #3

What did you do?

How did it work?

EXPLORE THE MYSTERY OBJECT
FOLLOW STEPS 1-2-3-4-5-6-7-8-9-10

Step 1 Teacher directions:

Step 2

_____   _____
Detective #1   Detective #2

Step 3 Look at the mystery object and talk about it.

Step 4 List four words that tell about the mystery object.

_____   _____

_____   _____

Step 5 Describe how it feels.

GA1396

MYSTERY OBJECT page 2

Step 6	What is this mystery object used for?

Step 7	Who would use this object?

Step 8	How does the mystery object work?

Step 9	Give the mystery object a name.

Step 10	Draw a picture of someone using the mystery object.

GA1396

YOU SOLVED THE MYSTERY

Name_____ Date _____

Teacher _____

A VERY CREATIVE GUESS

Name_____ Date _____

Teacher _____

GA1396

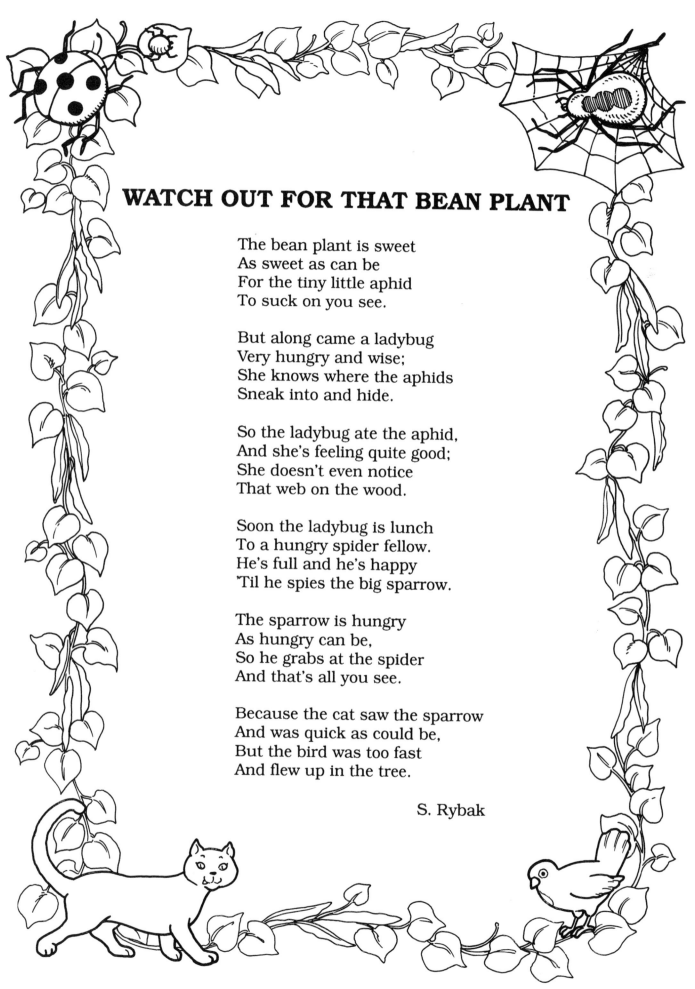

WATCH OUT FOR THAT BEAN PLANT

The bean plant is sweet
As sweet as can be
For the tiny little aphid
To suck on you see.

But along came a ladybug
Very hungry and wise;
She knows where the aphids
Sneak into and hide.

So the ladybug ate the aphid,
And she's feeling quite good;
She doesn't even notice
That web on the wood.

Soon the ladybug is lunch
To a hungry spider fellow.
He's full and he's happy
'Til he spies the big sparrow.

The sparrow is hungry
As hungry can be,
So he grabs at the spider
And that's all you see.

Because the cat saw the sparrow
And was quick as could be,
But the bird was too fast
And flew up in the tree.

S. Rybak

111

GA1396

FOOD CHAIN GAME RULES

Each player is part of a food chain. That means that one animal eats the next animal in order to survive. The animal that gets eaten is called the *prey,* and the animal that eats the other animal is called the *predator.*

This is our food chain.

The fava bean plant grows leaves.

The aphid sucks the juices from the leaf of the favia bean.

The ladybug eats the aphid.

The spider catches the ladybug in the web.

The bird eats the spider.

The cat catches the bird.

Each of these creatures needs the one above it on the food chain in order to survive.

Game Rules

Each player tosses one die. The lowest roller gets to play first and pick his/her game piece. If there is a tie, roll again.

The object of the game is to eat into the center of the web. The first player to reach the center is the winner.

If you land on the picture of a critter that eats you, you lose a turn.

If you land on the picture of a critter that you eat, you take an extra turn to roll the die and move.

The food chain is on the side of the board to help you remember.

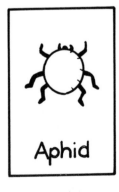
Aphid

Ladybug

Spider

Bird

GA1396

THE FOOD CHAIN

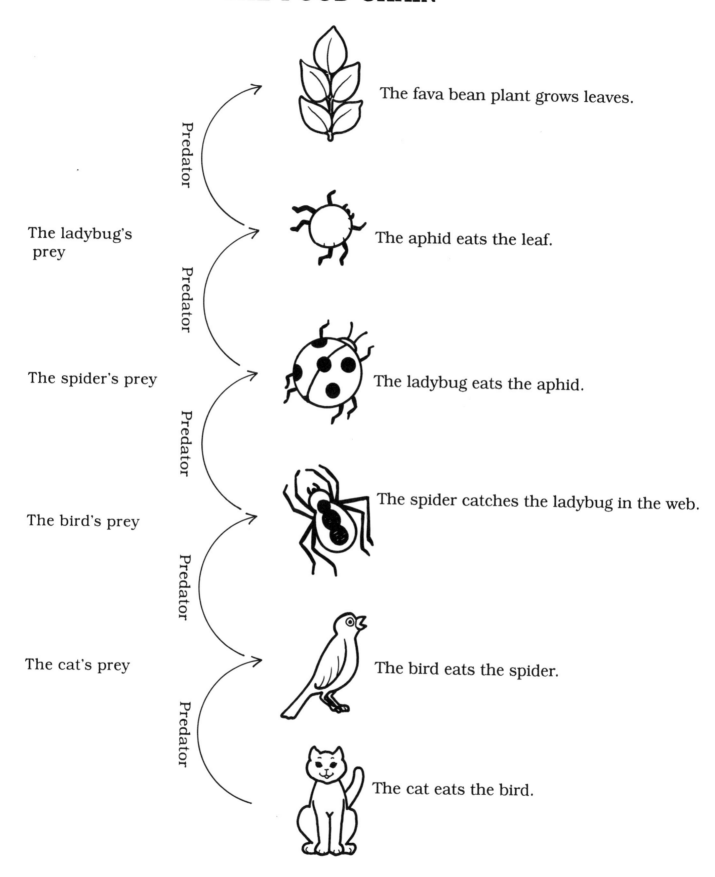

The fava bean plant grows leaves.

Predator

The ladybug's prey

Predator

The aphid eats the leaf.

The spider's prey

Predator

The ladybug eats the aphid.

The bird's prey

Predator

The spider catches the ladybug in the web.

The cat's prey

Predator

The bird eats the spider.

The cat eats the bird.

GA1396

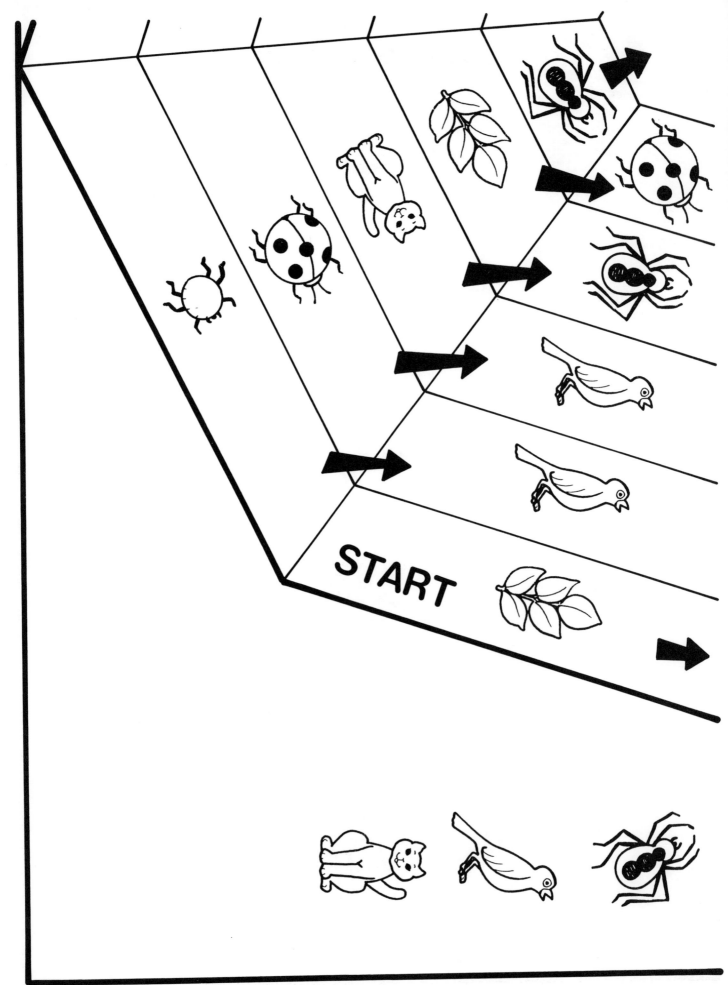

START

GA1396

115

the FOOD CHAIN Game

GA1396

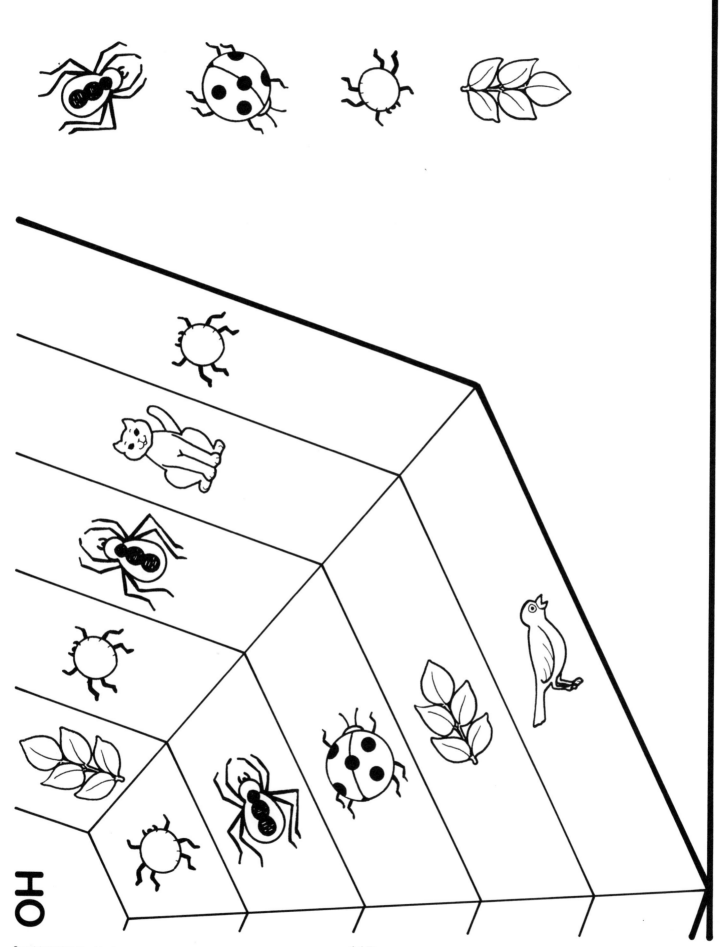

GA1396

ASSEMBLY LINES

The assembly line was considered to be one of the greatest additions to the Industrial Revolution. This was created at a time when the thinking prevailed that man was a machine. Exploring this concept with children can raise some interesting thoughts. Questions such as these may arise. Is it fun to do the same job all day, every day? What problems might arise from doing the same job? How did you feel when you had to stay at your job? How could the jobs still be done, but with more fun for the worker?

Mosaic Butterfly

In this activity, every child adds a piece to the butterfly to complete a mosaic picture. Each child will cut out the same colored piece and put it in the mosaic. You will need enough copies to have one for each child in your classroom. The puzzle has thirty available puzzle pieces. Pieces can be combined or divided based on the number of children in the classroom.

All the children are lined up on both sides of tables or desks. The children should have their pieces and a bottle of glue. Send the first paper through the assembly line and show the children how the process works. At this time take care of any problems, and then begin the assembly line.

When the butterflies are done, have the children talk about the problems that occurred on the line. What happened if someone was slow? What if a part was put in the wrong place? How did they feel after the last butterfly was made? Do they feel ownership to their butterfly?

Other Fun Assembly Lines

FIRST-AID KITS–The children can work together to create a first-aid kit for summer fun. It can include a Band-Aid, a safety pin, a bag, gauze and emergency phone numbers. Other materials can be added by the children.

BANANA DIPS–In this assembly line, the children need to peel the bananas, cut the bananas in half, put in the sticks, dip them in chocolate, roll them in sprinkles and wrap them in waxed paper.

RECYCLING CENTER–The children have to collect or be a center for the collection of plastic, paper and cans. The line will have the children crushing the plastic and cans and testing the cans with a magnet to see if they are steel or aluminum. Make sure everything is washed out beforehand.

GA1396

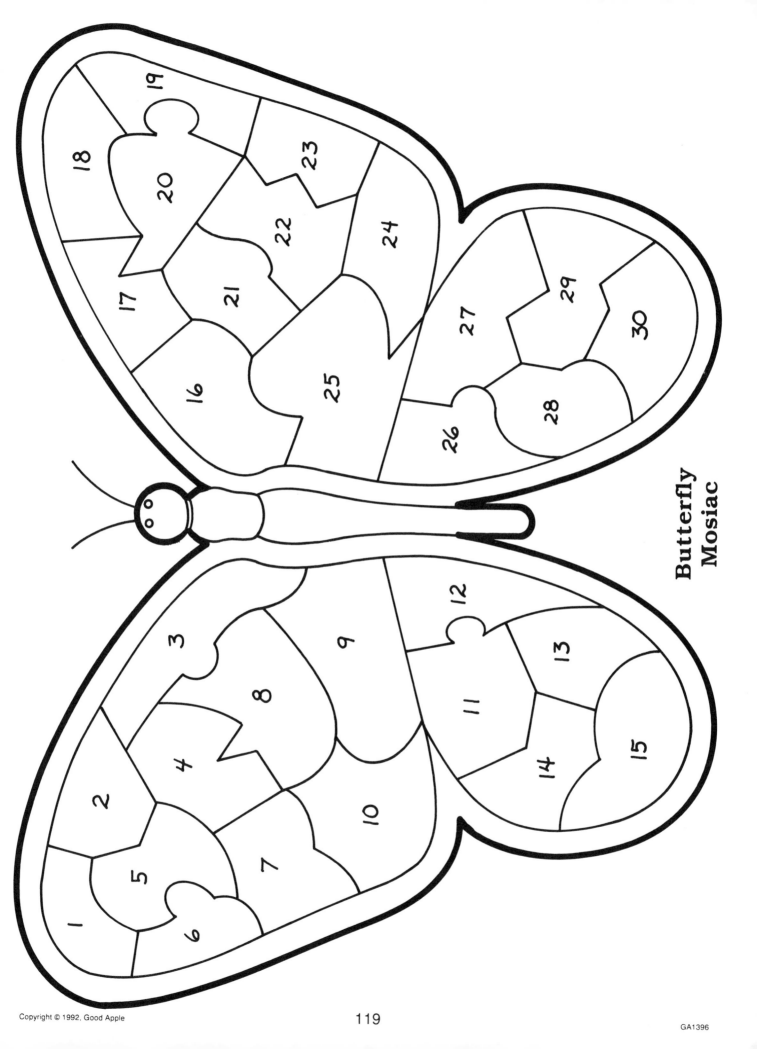

Butterfly Mosiac

119

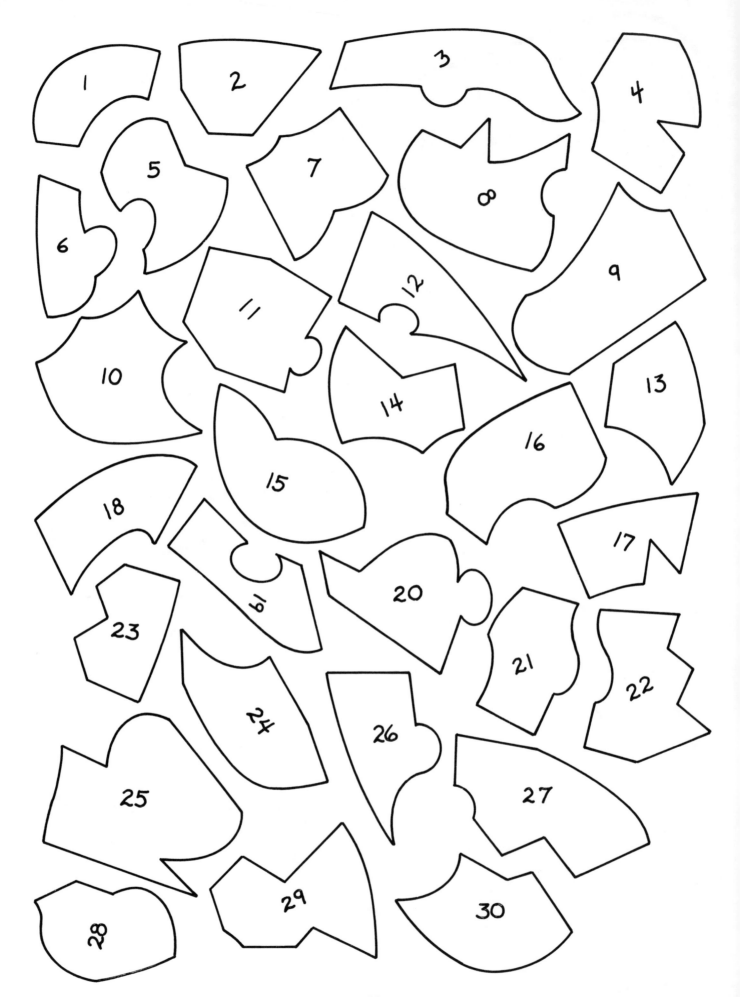

GA1396

PRESENTATION OF GROUP MATERIALS

I have found that children enjoy a finished product. Group work can provide some fun opportunities for an interesting presentation of the group's product. Groups of children can create a component of the finished product.

Flap Books

A class book is created when the children tell stories using the following format. Once upon a time... Then one day a funny thing happened... But in the end.... Each child gets a different part, and the book is put together so the children can mix and match the beginnings, middles and ends of the stories. Start with a central theme such as dog stories so the parts will all thread together. A small version of this book can be created, or a class book can be bound together.

Mobile Reports

The plastic bands that go around six-packs of soda pop are the bases for these mobiles. There are six rings. In each ring the children can tie their reports or art activities. Some sample pages have been included. Castles for fairy tale activities, haunted houses for Halloween, children for family or community units, bears for animal or bear activities and umbrellas for spring or rainy day fun are just a few of the possibilities. The children can work together on book reports, lab teams or exploration groups. When they are done, they can record their activities on the backs of these mobile figures and hang them in the room.

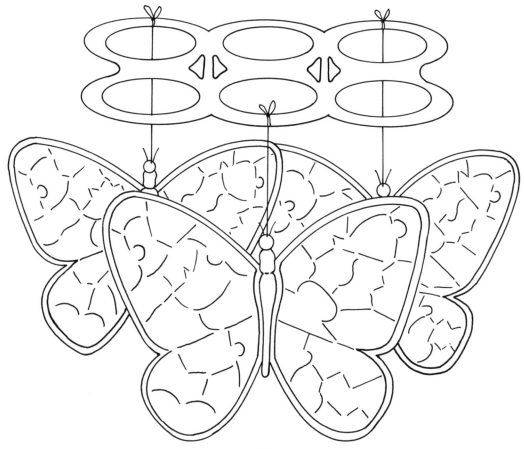

Once upon a time _____

_____

_____

_____

_____

_____

_____

_____

cut -

Then one day a funny thing happened _____

_____

_____

_____

_____

_____

_____

_____

_____

_____

cut -

But in the end _____

_____

_____

_____

_____

_____

_____

_____

_____

_____

122

GA1396

123

124

GA1396

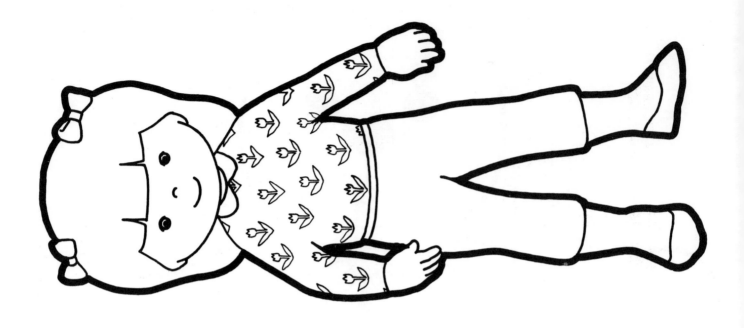

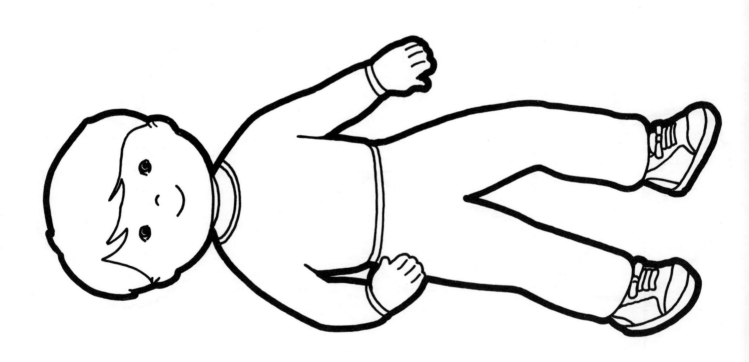

126

127

CHILDREN WORKING TOGETHER

It is my hope that this book has opened some doors to the directions children can use to effectively work together in your classroom. The possibilities for group work are endless. As a teacher, I have seen academic as well as interpersonal growth by using these methods. The classroom attitude is "We came to learn, so let's do it together." We all have a purpose and a mission.

I have overheard children discussing a particular unit they are studying. Children are asking if they could have some time to work with their group at 3:15 in the afternoon. Some children buddy study during indoor recess, and others will thoughtfully sit down and help another without being asked.

This is a room filled with respect for the individual and the family unit we have created. We all take ownership and pride in each other's accomplishments. The most touching moment came when one child tested out of a special program and was mainstreamed back into the classroom. The class burst into spontaneous applause for that child with cheers and verbal praise. Those are the moments you know something is going right!

One thing that I have noticed is that the children enjoy a creative and "pulled-together" look to their activities. They seem to maintain interest longer if the activity has a clever presentation. The final few pages of this book are a dozen and one suggestions for group presentation. These will hopefully get you thinking of many others.

Finally, trust your children. At first, the children may not be trusted to learn on their own because the system hasn't been set up to help children's innate learning, so pretend to trust them. Treat them like scientists or researchers in a think tank. Believe in their abilities, and magically they will show them to you.

There will always be setbacks. Children have learned that school is a place to do what you are told to do. In this new environment, the children grab the reins and run with their learning. Some of them may run to a corner to play. You will know these children immediately because they will be watching you. The children who are talking, busy and on task will not be watching you. The children who are watching you want a reaction or want to see if they will be in trouble. Some children may not be ready, and they may need to work alone. Not everyone can cooperate and work in groups, even as adults.

Just remember that this type of teaching is hard work, noisy and exciting! If children can sense the feeling of ownership for their learning, they are on the road to being lifelong learners. By stepping back and giving them a chance, we are giving them a gift of a lifetime.

A DOZEN AND ONE MORE IDEAS FOR GROUP PRESENTATIONS

The following ideas are a clever way to present group reports, individual journals, stories or activities.

The patterns can be enlarged on your copier or opaque projector.

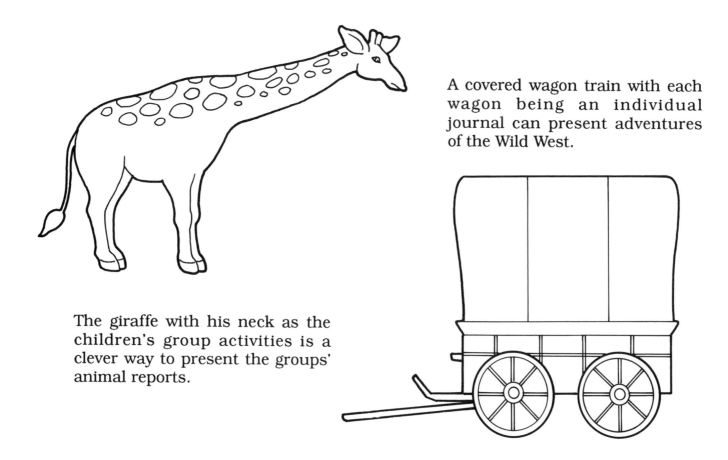

A covered wagon train with each wagon being an individual journal can present adventures of the Wild West.

The giraffe with his neck as the children's group activities is a clever way to present the groups' animal reports.

A giant train with many cars is another way for the children to complete their reports as a group.

129

GA1396

"The Princess and the Pea" story creates a chance for the children to make a giant pile of mattresses. Each mattress is a child's story or report. The children can retell familiar fairy tales and sequence the stories. A beautiful princess sits on the top of the mattresses.

Seals that balance balls provide a cute bulletin board that puts each project on a different color ball balanced from the seal's nose.

A bouquet of flowers with each flower center being the child's individual report or activity is a colorful way to present spring activities.

A forest of trees with different environmental information makes an attractive bulletin board.

GA1396

A basket of giant acorns makes a clever display. The children write or draw on the acorns and put the caps on when they are done.

Wise owls on a tree branch share information. The children can write on the owls and mount them on real tree branches.

A school of fish that float from hanging mobiles can present studies of aquatic life.

Eggs in a bird's nest can be a nice display for a study of birds and their habits.

A gaggle of geese running down the hallway is a popular way to present a group activity. The geese can even have bows tied around their necks for color.

Peas in a pod with each pea presenting a different piece of information on the group activity can be hung on the wall.

GA1396

COOPERATIVE LEARNING

Different children working together
Much the same way as adults.
Working to share and working to learn
Bending to create the results.

It's sometimes difficult and frustrating
The noise, the confusion, the pace.
But the end results make it worth it.
Together they all win the race.

We live in a world full of questions
And our children must answer them all.
They must find their way united.
Alone they will stumble and fall.

As teachers we all touch tomorrow
By planting the seeds every day.
Cooperative learning is one way
To improve a child's life in all ways.

So together they all will learn better.
This will carry them through when they're grown.
Together they create a tomorrow
They won't have to face all alone.

S. Rybak

GA1396